AF375213

BEYOND BITCOIN

UNLOCKING THE SECRETS OF CRYPTOCURRENCY

The Crypto Code Book

VIGNESSH B

Contents

PART 2   CONSENSUS MECHANISM

PART 3   TOKENOMICS

PART 4   BASICS 101: INVESTING IN CRYPTOCURRENCIES

PART 5   DYOR

Foreword

In this rapidly changing landscape of finance and technology, cryptocurrencies have emerged as a revolutionary force, challenging traditional concepts of money and financial systems. As a non-fiction writer delving into the complexities of finance and the digital currency revolution, my goal is to make these often misunderstood topics accessible and to provide readers with practical insights.

This book serves as a guide through the intricate world of cryptocurrencies, where innovation meets opportunity. We will embark on a journey to explore the origins of digital money, the underlying technologies, and their profound impact on global finance. Along the way, I will share stories of triumph and caution, highlight emerging trends, and offer practical advice for navigating this dynamic market.

Whether you are an experienced investor, an interested novice, or a financial professional seeking to better understand blockchain technology, this book is designed to equip you with the knowledge and tools needed to make informed decisions. Together, we will unravel complexities and embrace the possibilities at the intersection of finance and technology.

Thank you for joining me on this journey. Let's dive into the world of cryptocurrencies and unveil the future.

Copyright

Introduction

Unless you have been living in the 1900s, you have likely heard about Bitcoin and the term "cryptocurrencies." At the time of writing, more than 23,000 cryptocurrencies exist—six times more than when I first wrote my book, "Cryptocurrency for Beginners with Special Focus on Indian Market." The hype began in 2017 when Bitcoin's value increased by 1,318 percent, and it surged by 3,374,999,900% from its first recorded price in 2009. This rise was modest compared to Ripple, which surged by 36,018 percent. These returns far exceed what a stock investor could achieve in a lifetime, surpassing any other investment plan.

When the bubble popped in 2018, many investors who had bought cryptocurrencies at high prices suffered losses. As a result, many early investors branded the industry as a scam and returned to traditional assets such as stocks.

Cryptocurrencies are based on a recent technology called blockchain. Blockchain forms the infrastructure on which cryptocurrencies are built. While cryptocurrencies are one application of blockchain, many other uses can also be developed around this technology.

This book is for you if you're looking to understand what blockchains are, the basics of how to use them, which cryptocurrencies cryptocurrency.are good investments besides Bitcoin, and other ways of earning in cryptocurrency.

At the time of writing this book, BTC and ETH ETFs have been launched, marking a historical day in the world of cryptocurrencies. Bitcoin and Ethereum ETFs, or exchange-traded funds, are investment instruments that allow investors to gain exposure without having to physically hold cryptocurrencies. These ETFs are listed on traditional stock exchanges, helping institutional and retail investors include Bitcoin and Ethereum in their portfolios through a familiar, regulated framework. Bitcoin ETFs typically track the price of Bitcoin, and Ethereum ETFs track the price of Ether. This offers investors an indirect way to gain exposure to the potential upside of these digital assets without needing a cryptocurrency wallet or exchange account. The launch of these ETFs is seen as a significant step towards mainstreaming cryptocurrencies in financial markets, serving as a bridge between traditional finance and the new digital asset era.

Part 1

GETTING STARTED WITH CRYPTOCURRENCY

Chapter 1

Money & Economics

Before starting your cryptocurrency journey, let's comprehend what money is.

Paper money was first introduced in China during the 11th century and gradually spread to most of Europe by the 17th century. This transition was formalized with the establishment of institutions like the Bank of England in 1694.

Gold certificates were developed as a replacement for physical gold, making transactions easier. Backed by tangible gold reserves, these certificates represented a promise of redemption on demand, effectively bridging the gap between physical gold and paper currency.

Standard for Gold

The gold standard, the monetary system of relating currency to gold reserves, had been the order of the day in global economies for centuries. However, 1944's Bretton Woods Agreement heralded a new dawn by ditching the gold standard in favor of fiat currency.

Fiat currency

Fiat currency allows central banks the power to control monetary policy and economic stability. The US dollar became the world's reserve currency to be utilized in global trading and financial systems.

"Fiat" a Latin word meaning "let it be done" refers to government-issued currency that is only as valuable as the trust people have in the issuing authority. Contrary to commodity-backed currency, fiat money does not have intrinsic value but has to be acceptable based on trust in the government.

Central banks and governments wield unprecedented power and influence on economic policy on a fiat currency. They can, therefore, control money supply and inflation. However, it has always been subject to depreciation and inflationary tendencies, hence prone to economic instability.

World Reserve Currency

The USD was a world reserve currency following the United States' importance in World War II. The Bretton Woods Agreement is responsible for permanently fixing the dollar's position and exchange rates to enable global exchange.

Not everybody likes fiat currency despite its prominence. Following the 2008 economic crisis, Bitcoin emerged as a decentralized digital currency to address fiat models' challenges.

Evolution in Payments

Following the gold standard's demise, financial institutions introduced various payment innovations:

1. 1958: Bank of America introduced the BankAmericard, the precursor to modern credit cards.

2. 1967: The first ATM debuted at Barclay's Branch in Enfield, London, and transforming banking accessibility.

3. 1997: Sumitomo Bank pioneered online banking services, in the era of digital finance.

4. 2009: Bitcoin emerged as the world's first decentralized cryptocurrency.

5. 2013: Vancouver, Canada, saw the unveiling of the world's first publicly available Bitcoin ATM, marking the rise of digital currencies.

Regulations

Sound and healthy financial systems depend on stringent regulatory frameworks to ensure stability and integrity. Regulatory bodies such as the Financial Conduct Authority oversee market participants and enforce compliance with set laws and regulations. Government oversight is critical in protecting financial markets and consumers from fraud and misconduct. Regulatory reforms primarily aim to improve transparency, accountability, and systemic resilience in response to financial crises.

Economics

For a crypto investor, economics provides an edge by enabling rational decisions based on well-informed judgments about factors influencing cryptocurrency prices and market dynamics. Below is the role economics plays for a crypto investor:

Supply and Demand: Cryptocurrency, like any other asset, is governed by the laws of supply and demand. When the demand for a particular cryptocurrency increases while its supply remains constant, the price of the cryptocurrency rises. The opposite is true when demand decreases or supply increases. Economic principles guide investors in evaluating factors affecting supply and demand in the crypto market, such as changes in investor sentiment, regulatory developments, technological advancements, and macroeconomic trends.

Market Psychology: Economics includes studying human behavior and decision-making. Market psychology is particularly relevant as investor sentiment, speculative trends, and psychological factors like fear and greed impact cryptocurrency prices. Economic theories help investors spot market trends and make well-informed decisions based on market dynamics.

Macroeconomic Factors: Cryptocurrency prices are affected by macroeconomic factors such as inflation, interest rates, geopolitical events, and economic policies. For instance, during inflation threats, investors might seek alternative stores of value, turning to Bitcoin. In economic uncertainty, investors may also turn to cryptocurrencies for refuge. Investors need to understand macroeconomic trends and their potential effects on cryptocurrency markets.

Regulatory Environment: Economic policies and regulatory developments can influence the cryptocurrency market. Government regulations, tax policies, and legal frameworks impact investor confidence and market stability. Economic analysis helps investors anticipate regulatory changes and assess their implications on cryptocurrency prices and market dynamics.

Global Economic Trends: Trends in cryptocurrency markets are integrated with global financial markets and are vulnerable to broad economic trends and events. Leading economic indicators affecting investor sentiment include GDP growth, unemployment rates, and consumer spending. Economic analysis enables investors to recognize correlations between cryptocurrency prices and global economic trends, helping them make more informed investment decisions.

Micro and Macroeconomics

Microeconomics:

Microeconomics studies the economic behavior of individuals, households, and firms and the allocation and optimization of resources at a micro or individual level. It analyzes how individual consumers decide to purchase goods and services, how firms set prices, and how markets allocate resources. Topics include the relationship between supply and demand for goods and services, consumer behavior, production and costs, market structures (e.g., perfect competition, monopoly, oligopoly), and factors influencing decision-making such as utility and profit maximization.

In the case of cryptocurrencies, microeconomics analyzes how individual investors decide to buy or sell cryptocurrencies, how firms set prices for digital assets, and how changes in supply and demand for digital assets impact cryptocurrency prices on a smaller scale.

Macroeconomics

Macroeconomics examines the behavior of entire economies, focusing on aggregates such as national income, unemployment rates, inflation, and overall economic growth. It studies broader economic factors affecting the entire economy, including government policies, fiscal and monetary policies, international trade, and global economic trends. Macroeconomics seeks to understand the causes of long-term economic growth, business cycle fluctuations, and the determinants of aggregate demand and supply.

In the context of cryptocurrency, macroeconomics applies to how government regulations, central bank policies, and macroeconomic indicators influence the cryptocurrency market. For example, changes in interest rates or monetary policy can impact the investment climate, thereby affecting the demand for cryptocurrencies on a broad scale.

Supply and Demand

Law of Demand: All other things being equal, a higher price of a good leads to a lower quantity demanded by buyers, and vice versa. Higher prices strain buyers' limited resources, causing them to purchase less, while lower prices encourage them to buy more.

Law of Supply: All other things being constant, a higher price of a commodity results in a larger quantity supplied by sellers, and vice versa. Higher prices incentivize producers to supply more, as they can achieve greater profits.

Equilibrium Price: This is the price at which the demand for a product equals its supply. At this price, buyers are willing to purchase exactly the quantity that sellers are willing to sell, creating a balance between demand and supply.

While these laws provide a theoretical framework for analyzing market behavior, actual supply and demand influences can be complex, affected by factors such as consumer preferences, income levels, government policies, and technological advances. Price elasticity, meanwhile, highlights the sensitivity of the quantity demanded or supplied to price changes.

Inflation

Inflation measures the increase in the general price of goods and services over time, leading to a decrease in the purchasing power of money.

Causes of Inflation

1. Increase in Money Supply: An abrupt rise in currency circulation results in inflation as more money chases the same quantity of goods and services.

2. Demand-Pull Inflation: This occurs when the demand for goods and services exceeds their supply, pushing prices upward.

3. Cost-Push Inflation: An increase in production costs, such as labor or raw materials, is passed on to consumers, leading to higher prices.

4. Built-In Inflation: The expectation of future inflation leads to wage increases, which, in turn, raise the cost of goods and services, creating a vicious cycle of inflation.

Government and Central Bank Response

Monetary Policy: Central banks control inflation by regulating the money supply through interest rates. Lowering interest rates reduces borrowing costs, thereby curbing inflation. Conversely, raising interest rates decreases borrowing and spending, helping to lower inflation.

Fiscal Policy: The government influences economic activity through fiscal policy. By increasing taxes, the government reduces disposable income, lowering demand and, consequently, inflation.

Measurement: Inflation is measured by the Consumer Price Index (CPI), which tracks changes in the prices of a specific basket of goods and services purchased by consumers over time.

Consumer Price Index (CPI)

CPI tracks how the price consumers pay for a basket of goods and services changes over time. It is one of the essential measures of inflation or deflation in a country or region.

Used in Monetary Policy: Central banks, like the U. S. Federal Reserve, use CPI to design monetary policies. Monitoring CPI helps central banks decide on interest rates and other tools to control inflation or boost economic growth.

How it is computed: CPI is calculated as a weighted average of the cost of a basket of goods and services that consumers typically buy. This basket includes categories such as food, housing, transport, and education.

How the Data is collected: Price data is gathered for the items in the basket from retailers, service providers, and rental units. Prices of about 94,000 items are used to compute CPI, weighted according to their importance in the average consumer's expenditure patterns.

Formula: The formula for calculating CPI is:

CPI= (C–PP) ×100CPI= (PC–P) ×100

Where:

CC is the current price of the representative basket.

PP is the price in the base period.

Example: Suppose the basket of goods and services costs $2,100 in the base year of 2023 and $2,250 in 2024. The CPI calculation will be:

CPI= (2,250–2,100)/2,100) ×100=7.14

This indicates that the CPI for the period from 2023 to 2024 is 7.14, meaning prices increased by 7.14%.

Gross Domestic Product (GDP)

GDP is the total market value of finished goods and services produced within a region's boundaries during a certain period. It measures the economic performance of a country, making it the best gauge of a nation's economic health and growth.

Types of GDP:

1. Nominal GDP: Measures the value of goods and services at current market prices without considering inflation, reflecting economic output in monetary terms for the current year.

2. Real GDP: Accounts for inflation by measuring the quantity of goods and services produced, providing a better reflection of economic growth or contraction over time.

3. GDP per Capita: Measures economic output per citizen, indicating the average standard of living within a country.

Calculation:

The Expenditure Approach is a primary method used to calculate GDP, represented by the formula:

$C + G + I + NX = GDP$

C = Consumption (all consumer spending)

G = Government spending (e.g. payroll, infrastructure, and equipment)

I = Investment (all private domestic investment and capital expenditures)

NX = Net exports (all expenditures by companies located in a given country, even if they are foreign companies, are included)

Calculation of Real GDP: It is calculated using a price deflator, which adjusts for price changes between the base year and the current year. This allows economists to measure changes in economic output considering inflation or deflation.

GDP Growth Rate: The real GDP growth rate shows changes in real GDP over time as a percentage, measuring economic expansion or contraction and the pace of economic growth.

Riddles:

Supply and Demand Puzzle:

In a small town, there are two competing ice cream shops. One day, the price of milk increases significantly. How would this affect the supply and demand curves for ice cream in this town? What would likely happen to the price and quantity of ice cream sold?

Inflation Calculation:

If the consumer price index (CPI) was 200 last year and is 220 this year, what is the inflation rate? Show your calculation.

Currency Exchange Puzzle:

You are traveling from the United States to Europe and need to exchange your dollars for euros. If the exchange rate is 1 USD = 0.85 EUR, and you have $1000, how many euros will you receive? If the exchange rate changes to 1 USD = 0.80 EUR, how many euros would you receive for the same amount of dollars?

Chapter 2

Basics of Cryptocurrency

History of Cryptocurrency

The first-ever cryptocurrency created was Bitcoin. Bitcoin was the first product of blockchain technology, developed by the anonymous Satoshi Nakamoto in 2008. It was described as a peer-to-peer (P2P) version of electronic money.

Cryptocurrencies are created through a process called mining, which differs significantly from mining ore. Mining cryptocurrency requires powerful computers to solve complex problems. Bitcoin remained the only cryptocurrency until 2011. After that, developers created alternative coins, known as altcoins, to address perceived flaws in Bitcoin.

Key Crypto Benefits

With great power comes great responsibility. Still not convinced that cryptocurrencies are better than traditional government-controlled money? Here are the benefits a decentralized network can provide:

1. Eliminating the costs associated with money printing.

2. Giving people control over their money.

3. Cutting out the middlemen.

4. Reducing corruption.

5. Providing a secure mode of fund transfer.

Cryptography

Cryptography is the mathematical or computational practice of hiding or encrypting data. To understand cryptocurrency, it is essential to first understand cryptography. Simply put, it enables the safe transmission of messages between parties. The sender encrypts the message before transmission, and the recipient decrypts it to understand the original content.

This cryptographic process is the backbone of blockchain technology, ensuring safe transactions through a digital ledger without intermediaries. A blockchain serves as an online ledger, recording all transactions over time. Cryptography also verifies the authenticity of data.

The need for cryptography is crucial due to the recent growth in data accessibility for various technical reasons. While increased accessibility has many advantages, it also exposes data to risks such as malpractice, malicious attacks, and cyberattacks. Cryptography protects data through encryption.

Cryptocurrency is built on cryptographic principles. Introduced in 2009 by Satoshi Nakamoto on a cryptography message board, it aimed to create a new form of electronic payment based on cryptographic proof rather than trust. This system allows two parties to transact directly, eliminating the need for a trusted third party.

Using cryptography, blockchains enable secure and anonymous digital transactions without intermediaries. This cryptographic approach facilitates trustless cryptocurrency transactions, allowing users to securely complete transactions without knowing the other party.

According to economic times, "Cryptography is associated with the process of converting ordinary plain text into unintelligible text and vice versa. It is a method of storing and transmitting data in a particular form that only those from whom it is intended can read and process."

The term "cryptocurrency" is a misnomer. Many cryptocurrencies do not function as actual currencies; "crypto assets" is a more accurate term. Crypto assets have diverse functions based on their design. Some excel as a medium of exchange, some are inherently useful, and others provide governance access.

On the other hand, a crypto token is an asset that exists on a protocol, such as SOL on Solana. In the crypto world, "token" typically refers to any digital asset running on another cryptocurrency's blockchain. For example, many decentralized finance tokens fall into this category.

It's essential to distinguish between tokens and cryptocurrencies: a token is an application built on top of blockchains like Bitcoin or Ethereum, while a cryptocurrency is an integral part of a blockchain.

Understanding the history of cryptocurrencies, the role of cryptography, and the difference between cryptocurrencies and tokens enhances our perception of the digital assets shaping the future of finance.

Keep a watch:

Here are some cryptocurrencies to watch out for in the DePIN sector:

1. EMC Protocol - $EMC

2. Render Network - $RNDR

3. Ator Protocol - $ATOR

4. Akash Network - $AKT

Not financial advice, but these are just my personal favorites and are for learning purposes.

Understanding the Basics of Blockchain

Understanding Blockchain

Many people are more familiar with Bitcoin than they are with blockchain. Some who are aware of blockchain believe it solely serves as the technology behind Bitcoin. While Bitcoin is one of the most well-known applications of blockchain technology, blockchain has the potential for much more. It could possibly be one of the most disruptive technologies in decades and could have a lasting impact on our lives.

Source: Patriot Software

What is Blockchain?

At its most basic level, blockchain is an indelible online ledger that records every transaction in real-time for any cryptocurrency. It's considered one of the most secure ways of keeping a log of transactions or investments. This peer-to-peer technology requires every computer in the blockchain network to be in consensus about a particular transaction and to keep a copy of those transaction details, thus avoiding any chances of fraud.

Why is it Called Blockchain?

The term "blockchain" was first coined by Satoshi Nakamoto, the mysterious inventor of Bitcoin and blockchain. Nakamoto described it as "A Peer-to-Peer Electronic Cash System." All transactions are stored in a chronological chain, with each new transaction assigned a unique hash number linking it to preceding and succeeding transactions. This chaining of data makes it highly fraud-resistant because altering any transaction would disrupt the entire sequence. Additionally, since every transaction requires network-wide approval, it secures the system from any external interference.

Traditional Banking vs. Blockchain

Unlike traditional banking, where transactions are bound by regulatory requirements and government interference, blockchain operates autonomously in the digital world. Users can send payments wherever they want for very small fees, without third-party involvement. Users have flexibility in choosing when and how much to pay, and which cryptocurrencies to use, making it a highly flexible method of sending money, from daily purchases to investments.

Security of Blockchain

Blockchain is renowned for its security. All transactions must be verified by everyone on the network and are permanently recorded in the ledger; even the smallest alteration would be obvious and difficult to carry out. Users can remain anonymous because cryptocurrencies exist in digital "wallets" without identifiers. Although this anonymity has attracted criminal activity, the system's security makes fraud nearly impossible.

Security Concerns in the Future

There are concerns that future technologies, such as quantum computing, might one day compromise the security of the blockchain system by altering transactions before they are logged. However, these threats are expected to be curtailed by improvements in blockchain technology and the use of artificial intelligence to monitor and identify fraud.

Advantages of Blockchain over Traditional Payment Systems

One of the central attractions of blockchain-based cryptocurrency payments is the speed of transactions. In virtually no time, transactions are complete—roughly about ten times quicker than regular bank transfers. Cryptocurrencies such as Ripple XRP can even compete with conventional interbank transfer systems such as SWIFT, offering much better efficiency and safety as the system is adopted more widely.

Disadvantages and Criticisms of Blockchain

Not everything is rosy about blockchain, however:

1. Energy Consumption: The process of new block creation is energy-intensive, raising concerns about sustainability.

2. Data Storage: The blockchain ledger can grow to a substantial size, requiring significant storage and potentially lengthening download times.

3. Limited Adoption: The number of people using cryptocurrencies and blockchain is relatively small compared to users of traditional payment methods like Visa and Mastercard. However, adoption is growing steadily.

4. Anonymity Issues: While anonymity is a strong feature, it's not foolproof. Tracking tools can potentially identify user patterns, compromising privacy.

5. Lack of Universal Protocols: Economist Nouriel Roubini argues that there are no universal protocols for blockchain, unlike the Internet, making widespread implementation challenging.

Despite these challenges, the volume of transactions using blockchain and cryptocurrencies continues to grow, and adoption is on the rise. Blockchain is likely to become an essential part of the global financial system as the value and usage of cryptocurrencies increase.

Checking Transactions on the Blockchain

As a cryptocurrency trader, learning how to trace your transactions on the blockchain is crucial. When you initiate a transaction, it undergoes several stages before execution, and you can monitor its progress using various applications and websites.

Understanding Confirmations

A "confirmation" refers to the recording of the transaction on the blockchain, permanently fixed there. Confirmations serve as proof that the funds have been credited to the correct address. The number of confirmations indicates the number of blocks built on top of the block recording your transaction. Typically, 6 confirmations are required for a transaction to be fully validated, with the coins appearing in the recipient's address. However, some platforms, like Coinbase, may require just 3 confirmations.

Tracking Transactions

To track a transaction, you'll need the transaction ID (Tx ID). Input this ID into a blockchain explorer to view the current status and details of the transaction. The choice of explorer depends on the blockchain network you're using. Here are some popular sites for checking transactions on different blockchains:

Bitcoin Transactions:

- Blockchain.info: A widely used Bitcoin blockchain explorer.
- Blockcypher: Another reliable Bitcoin explorer with additional features.

Ethereum Transactions:

- Etherscan: The most popular explorer for tracking Ethereum transactions and accessing detailed information about the Ethereum blockchain.
- Ethplorer: Another useful tool for Ethereum transactions.

Other Cryptocurrencies:

- CoinMarketCap: Provides links to explorers for various cryptocurrencies.
- Blockchair: Supports multiple cryptocurrencies beyond Bitcoin and Bitcoin Cash.

How to Track Transaction:

Obtain the Transaction ID (Tx ID) from your wallet or the exchange from which the transaction was sent.

Visit the appropriate blockchain explorer based on the cryptocurrency used.

Enter the Tx ID in the explorer's search bar.

Review the transaction details, including the number of confirmations, transaction time, and the recipient's address.

By familiarizing yourself with these tools and tracking your transactions, you can ensure the safe movement of your money and proper recording on the blockchain.

Blockchain Layers

Blockchain Scalability

Blockchain scalability refers to a blockchain network's ability to handle an increased volume of transactions. The growing adoption of cryptocurrencies has underscored the importance of blockchain scalability to maintain system security and ensure efficient transaction processing.

For instance, Bitcoin's main chain is limited to seven transactions per second (TPS), whereas the Visa network can handle over

20,000 TPS. Layer 2 (L2) blockchain technologies have been developed to automate transactions through smart contracts, thereby enhancing scalability without compromising security.

Importance of Blockchain Scalability

Scalability allows blockchain networks to accommodate more users and transactions. However, blockchain technology faces a challenge known as the trilemma, where optimizing decentralization, security, and scalability simultaneously is difficult. Increased demand can lead to higher transaction costs, deterring potential users. Layer one and layer two technologies aim to address these challenges and enhance network functionality.

Overview of Blockchain Layers

Blockchain layers, comprising various components in a blockchain architecture, facilitate secure and scalable network operations. There are four blockchain layers:

Layer 0:

- Components: The internet, hardware, and connections supporting blockchain networks.
- Function: Provides the foundational infrastructure for blockchain network operation.

Layer 1:

- Components: Root blockchain network, including consensus mechanisms, programming languages, block times, and dispute resolution.
- Function: Ensures the security and immutability of the core blockchain layer. Examples include Bitcoin and Ethereum.

Layer 2:

- Components: Third-party integrations like state channels, side chains, and rollups.
- Function: Enhances scalability by processing transactions off-chain and then recording results on the main blockchain (Layer 1), thus improving transaction speed and volume.

Layer 3:

- Components: Decentralized applications (dApps) and smart contracts.
- Function: Provides practical applications interacting with users and built atop blockchain networks.

Layer 4:

- Components: User interfaces and applications such as browsers and wallets.
- Purpose: Facilitates direct user communication with the blockchain network.

Differences between Blockchain Layers

Differences Between Blockchain Layers

Layer	Components	Function
Layer 0	Internet, hardware, connections	Provides fundamental infrastructure
Layer 1	Core blockchain network	Ensures security and immutability; handles consensus, block duration, dispute resolution
Layer 2	State channels, sidechains, rollups	Enhances scalability; processes transactions off-chain
Layer 3	dApps, smart contracts	Provides practical applications for user interaction
Layer 4	User interfaces, wallets	Facilitates end-user interaction with blockchain networks

Importance and Implementation

Layer 0: The basic technology behind the operations at all higher layers.

Layer 1: Provides for the security and immutability of the blockchain.

Layer 2: Addresses the issue of scalability by creating an off-chain so that transactions can be done off the chain with higher throughput.

Layer 3: Where applications reside, which actually make the blockchain technology useful and accessible for users.

Layer 4: The interfaces for users to interact with and engage in activities based on blockchain applications.

The understanding of these layers, how they relate, and combine is key for anyone engaged in learning blockchain since it can well explain the different levels of complexity and innovative solutions that make modern blockchain systems so resilient and scalable.

Do This:

Note Down!

What are the mistakes you've been making with cryptocurrencies?

What Layer does Bitcoin come under?

What Layer does MATIC come under?

Is Blockchain good or bad?

Chapter 4

Smart Contracts & Decentralised Applications (DApps)

What Are Smart Contracts?

Smart contracts are digital protocols created in code and stored on a blockchain. These protocols automatically execute and enforce the performance of a contract without third-party involvement, resembling traditional legal contracts but managed by code.

Key Characteristics:

- Automation: Pre-programmed terms are automatically enforced.
- Immutability: Contracts, once deployed on the blockchain, cannot be altered, ensuring security and trust.
- Transparency: Contract terms are publicly available on a blockchain.
- No Middlemen: Direct interaction between parties, eliminating intermediaries.

How Do Smart Contracts Work?

Smart contracts operate on the "if-then" model, where conditions trigger actions. For example:

Simple Example: "If $100 is deposited, then $5 is paid back daily for 24 days."

Complex Example: "If $100 is deposited, then $5 is paid back daily in Bitcoin and 6% interest in Ether."

Parties agree to terms, and the contract executes if conditions are met. Code verifies parties' ability to fulfill the agreement and executes transactions automatically.

Use Cases of Smart Contracts:

- Digital Agreements: Automate crypto transfers, enabling direct transactions without intermediaries.
- DeFi (Decentralized Finance): Power decentralized exchanges (DEX) for automated trades and limit orders.
- Web3 Applications: Support decentralized applications (DApps) across various platforms.

Benefits of Smart Contracts:

- Security: Cryptographic security ensures tamper-proof records.
- Autonomy: Automatic operation reduces manual involvement.
- Transparency: Contract terms and actions are visible on a blockchain.
- Cost-Efficiency: Eliminating intermediaries reduces transaction costs and processing time.

Weaknesses of Smart Contracts:

- Immutability: Inability to alter deployed contracts may pose challenges for error correction or future updates.
- Security Risks: Poorly written code can lead to vulnerabilities, emphasizing the need for proper design and security testing.

Smart contracts revolutionize blockchain and decentralized finance by automating agreements and eliminating middlemen, offering secure, transparent, and efficient solutions. However, sound design and security considerations are crucial to mitigate risks and ensure successful implementation.

Decentralised Applications (DApps)

Decentralized Applications, or DApps, function similarly to regular apps but operate within blockchain networks. They serve various real-world purposes and possess distinct features compared to traditional applications.

Features of DApps:

Open-Source:

Transparency: DApps are typically open-source, allowing anyone to access and review the code for verification and trust.

Smart Contracts:

Automation: DApps utilize smart contracts, enabling automated transactions with terms directly coded into the blockchain.

Decentralization:

User Control: Built on decentralized blockchain networks, DApps are controlled by users or individual nodes rather than a central authority.

Cryptographic Security:

Data Integrity: Secured using cryptographic technology, DApps store data on public blockchains, ensuring tamper-proof records without a single point of failure.

DApps vs. Traditional Apps:

Open Source Nature:

DApps: Open-source code fosters trust and safety within the community by allowing users to verify functionality and security.

Traditional Apps: Proprietary code limits transparency, forcing users to trust service providers without visibility into code operations.

Decentralization:

DApps: Operate on distributed networks, preventing centralized control and enhancing security through cryptographic measures.

Traditional Apps: Run on centralized servers, making them susceptible to vulnerabilities and potential data breaches.

Technical Problems and Vulnerability to Attacks:

DApps: Resilient to technical problems and attacks due to decentralized nature, though still susceptible to exploits if smart contract code is not properly audited.

Traditional Apps: Vulnerable to central server breaches, potentially leading to service disruptions and data loss.

Transparency and Trust:

DApps: Open-source code instills trust through transparency, allowing users to inspect and verify operations without reliance on a central authority.

Traditional Apps: Closed source limits transparency, necessitating trust in service providers for application functionality and security.

Control and Security:

DApps: Resilient against tampering with decentralized control and cryptographic security measures.

Traditional Apps: Vulnerable to centralized control and require robust security measures to safeguard data.

Robustness and Resilience:

DApps: Less vulnerable to single points of failure and network disruptions due to decentralized architecture.

Traditional Apps: Prone to single points of failure, making them susceptible to complete shutdowns in the event of attacks or technical glitches.

Mainnet vs. Testnet:

Mainnet:

Definition: Mainnet refers to the fully deployed and operational version of a blockchain or protocol, where transactions involving real value are processed.

Functionality: All functions of the blockchain network are live on the mainnet, and transactions conducted here involve real economic value, recorded on a public ledger.

Development Stage: While the mainnet represents the ultimate stage of a blockchain, ongoing iteration and updates are typical to enhance performance, security, and scalability.

Testnet:

Definition: Testnet serves as a blockchain or protocol in its development or testing phase, providing a sandbox environment for developers to test the network, identify bugs, and troubleshoot before launching on the mainnet.

Functionality: Transactions on a testnet do not involve real economic value and are often simulated using test tokens, allowing developers to experiment without risk to real user funds.

Development Stage: Testnets are crucial for ensuring the smooth operation of a blockchain or protocol before its deployment on the mainnet.

Advantages of DApps:

- Resiliency to Attacks: DApps are less susceptible to technical issues and attacks compared to centralized applications, as the decentralized nature of DApps ensures network continuity even if some nodes fail.
- Censorship Resistance: DApps are resistant to censorship, making it difficult for governments or powerful entities to regulate or block user access to the network.

- Trustless Operations: Users do not need to rely on a central authority, as blockchain technology and smart contracts ensure transaction integrity and correctness.

Disadvantages of DApps:

- Maintenance Challenges: Once deployed on the blockchain, updating or maintaining DApps becomes complex, requiring network consensus for any necessary change, which can be slow and cumbersome.
- User Experience: DApps may offer a less intuitive user experience compared to traditional applications, often requiring users to have a better understanding of blockchain technology and digital wallets.

Use Cases of DApps:

DApps find applications across various industries, including:

- Gaming: DApps provide ownership of in-game assets and enable trading within gaming ecosystems.
- Crypto Wallets: Secure storage and management of cryptocurrencies.
- DeFi (Decentralized Finance) Apps: Financial services such as lending, borrowing, and trading without intermediaries.
- Social Media: Platforms where users have control over their data and content.
- Decentralized Exchanges (DEXs): Trading cryptocurrencies without a central authority.

DApps represent a significant advancement in applications, leveraging blockchain technology to offer increased security, decentralization, and transparency. Despite facing challenges in maintenance and user experience, their advantages in resilience and censorship resistance make them valuable across gaming, finance, social media, and other sectors.

Part 2
CONSENSUS MECHANISM

Chapter 5

Nodes & Mining

What Is a Node?

A node is an electronic device operating within the blockchain network and is responsible for keeping and validating the decentralized ledger. A node could refer to different devices, including computers, cell phones, or even printers—essentially, any device that connects to the internet and joins the blockchain network. Each node has a copy of the blockchain and participates in the work of verifying and recording transactions.

What Is Mining?

Mining is the process through which nodes verify transactions and add them to the blockchain. It includes solving complex cryptographic puzzles, which require much computational power. Miners are incentivized individuals or entities running such nodes to receive a reward in the form of transaction fees and cryptocurrency.

How Mining Works

- Validation of Transactions:
    - When transactions take place, they are collected into blocks. These blocks are then broadcast to the nodes.

- Solving Puzzles:
    - Miners use software to solve the cryptographic puzzles connected with each block. It includes creating a large number of potential solutions, or hashes, until a correct one is found.

- Addition to the Blockchain:
    - The first miner to solve the puzzle has the right to add the block of transactions to the blockchain. Such miner is then rewarded with newly minted cryptocurrency and any transaction fees from the transactions within the block.

- Consensus Mechanism:
    - For the security and correctness of the blockchain, there is used a consensus mechanism. One such is the Proof-of-Work, where the difficulty of the puzzles will be such that adding a new block is not easy—a lot of computational work is needed to do that.

Challenges of Mining

Energy Consumption

Mining, especially in PoW systems like Bitcoin, uses powerful computers to solve complex puzzles, hence the need for much energy. It has raised concerns about its environmental implications.

Centralization Risks

It is observed that if a few large entities hold a significant portion of the network's computational power, mining could become centralized. This will result in them having undue influence over the network.

Hardware Requirements:

Effective mining requires specialized hardware, often called ASICs (Application-Specific Integrated Circuits), which are expensive and consume a lot of power.

Mining in Different Cryptocurrencies

Bitcoin and PoW:

Bitcoin is the most well-known cryptocurrency that uses the PoW consensus mechanism. In Bitcoin mining, miners compete to solve puzzles, and the first to do so adds a new block to the blockchain and earns Bitcoin as a reward.

Non-Mineable Cryptocurrencies:

Not all cryptocurrencies can be mined. For example, Ripple (XRP) does not use mining. Instead, it uses a more energy-efficient consensus protocol.

What is Consensus Mechanism?

A consensus mechanism is the method by which a blockchain network verifies and validates transactions. Unlike centralised systems, where a central authority manages and updates the database, blockchains operate in a decentralised manner. This decentralisation necessitates a system to ensure all participants, or 'nodes,' agree on the validity of transactions and data added to the blockchain.

Purpose of Consensus Mechanisms:

- Verification: Ensure that transactions added to the blockchain are accurate and genuine.
- Security: Protect the network from malicious activities and attacks.
- Decentralisation: Maintain the network without relying on a central authority.
- Agreement: Achieve consensus among distributed nodes on the state of the blockchain.

Consensus mechanisms are crucial because they enable trust and coordination in a decentralised environment, ensuring the blockchain operates smoothly and securely.

Types of Consensus Mechanisms

Different blockchains use various consensus mechanisms, each with unique principles and methods. Here are three of the most common:

- Proof-of-Work (PoW)
- Proof of Stake (PoS)
- Proof of History (PoH)

Other types of Consensus mechanisms are

- Proof-of-Authority (PoA)
- Proof-of-importance(PoI)

Chapter 6

Proof of Work (PoW)

Proof of Work (PoW) is a consensus mechanism used by many cryptocurrencies, including Bitcoin, to ensure the integrity and security of the blockchain. In PoW, miners compete to add new blocks to the blockchain by solving complex mathematical problems. This process involves producing proof that is difficult to create but easy for others to verify.

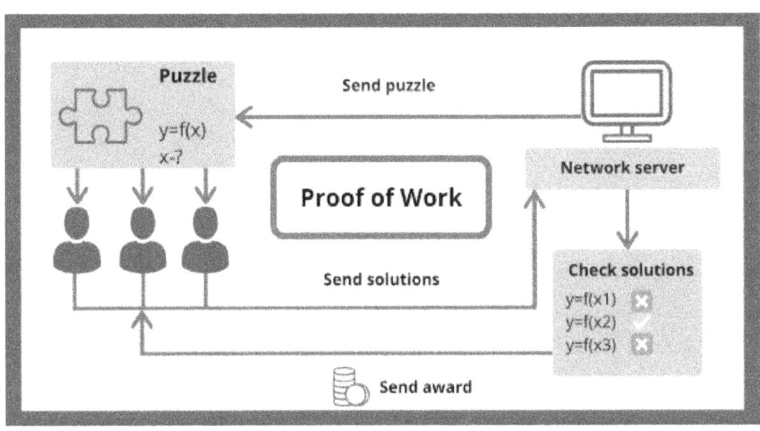

Source: Web 3 Labs

How PoW Works

Challenge and Proof

Challenge: The problem involves solving a cryptographic puzzle that requires significant computational effort and resources.

Proof: The solution to the puzzle serves as proof that the required work has been done. This proof is easily verifiable by other network nodes.

Example: Guess a Combination

Imagine trying to guess the combination of a lock. You must attempt many possible combinations to find the correct one, which is difficult and time-consuming. However, verifying the correct combination is simple—just try it in the lock.

Reward System

- The first miner to solve the problem and provide valid proof gets to add their block of transactions to the blockchain.
- The winning miner receives a cryptocurrency reward, such as Bitcoin, incentivizing miners to continue participating in the network.

PoW Advantages

- **Security:** The high computational work required makes it difficult and costly for attackers to tamper with the blockchain.
- **Decentralization:** PoW supports decentralization, allowing any node with sufficient computational resources to participate in mining.

PoW Disadvantages

- **High Energy Consumption:** PoW requires substantial computing power and electricity, leading to a large carbon footprint and high operational costs.
- **Scalability:** The intensive computational requirements limit the scalability of the network.

Principle

Nodes (miners) compete to solve complex mathematical puzzles. The first to solve the puzzle gets to add a new block to the blockchain and is rewarded with cryptocurrency.

Example: Bitcoin and Ethereum (until Ethereum 2.0).

Although Proof of Work was considered a promising method for ensuring the security and reliability of early blockchains like Bitcoin, its high energy consumption and scalability issues have been problematic. Consequently, alternative mechanisms such as Proof of Stake (PoS) have emerged. The general trend in new consensus mechanisms is to address PoW's limitations while maintaining decentralization and security principles

Chapter 7

Proof of Stake (PoS)

Proof of Stake (PoS) is a consensus mechanism developed as an alternative to Proof of Work (PoW) to address its high energy consumption and scalability issues. In PoS, validators are selected based on the amount of cryptocurrency they own and are willing to "stake" as collateral.

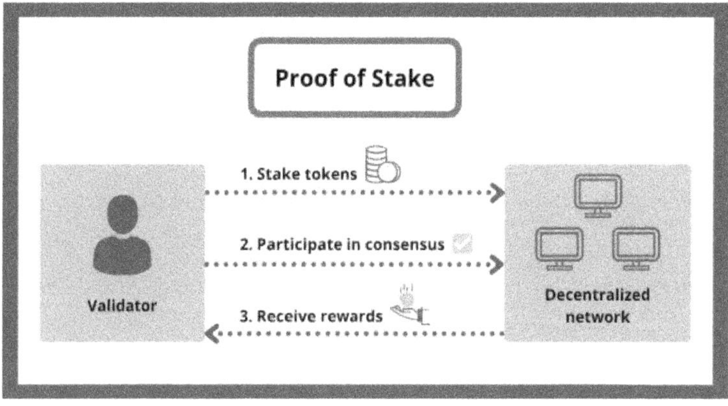

Source: Web 3 Labs

How Does PoS Work?

Stake-Based Selection:

- **Selection Process:** Validators are chosen to propose and validate new blocks based on the amount of cryptocurrency they own and stake. The more crypto a validator stakes, the higher their chances of being selected.

- **Environmental Impact:** This method does not require energy-intensive computations, making it more environmentally friendly.

Validation and Rewards:

- **Transaction Fees:** Validators in PoS earn transaction fees from the transactions they validate instead of block rewards. This approach eliminates the need for expensive mining hardware and high electricity costs.

Security and Efficiency:

- **Collateral:** Validators must lock up a certain amount of cryptocurrency as collateral, which they can lose if they validate fraudulent transactions. This creates an economic incentive to act honestly.

Advantages of PoS

- **Energy Efficiency:** PoS is much less energy-intensive compared to PoW, making it more sustainable and environmentally friendly.
- **Cost Efficiency:** PoS reduces the need for expensive mining equipment and high electricity bills, cutting down on the cost of running the network.
- **Scalability:** PoS can handle higher transaction throughput, making the blockchain more scalable.

Examples of PoS Blockchains

- **Polkadot (DOT):** A multi-chain network that allows various blockchains to interoperate.

- **Avalanche (AVAX):** A platform for creating decentralized applications and custom blockchain networks.
- **Cardano (ADA):** A blockchain platform for smart contracts, similar to Ethereum.

Criticisms of PoS

- **Wealth Concentration:** PoS tends to advantage individuals who already own significant amounts of cryptocurrency. Validators with more staked coins have a higher probability of being chosen to validate transactions, potentially leading to centralization of power.
- **Economic Incentives:** The PoS model might encourage validators to hoard their coins instead of spending them, as holding a larger stake increases their chances of being selected to validate blocks and earn transaction fees. This can reduce market liquidity.
- **Rich Get Richer:** Wealthy holders will accumulate more gains in terms of transaction fees and continue increasing their coin holdings. This can result in wealth concentration in the hands of a few validators, granting them disproportionate power over the network.

Principle

Validators are selected based on the number of coins they hold and are willing to "stake" as collateral. The more coins staked, the higher the chances of being selected to validate transactions and create new blocks.

Proof of Stake offers a more efficient and scalable alternative to Proof of Work but is not without its challenges, such as wealth accumulation and economic incentives. Ongoing developments in the blockchain space aim to address these issues and provide further improvements to PoS, ensuring the security and efficiency of decentralized networks.

Delegated Proof of Stake (DPoS)

Delegated Proof of Stake (DPoS) is an enhancement of the Proof of Stake (PoS) consensus model, designed to improve efficiency and democratize the process. In DPoS, stakeholders vote to elect a number of delegates who are given the power to validate transactions and create new blocks on their behalf, thus streamlining and making the process more scalable.

How Does DPoS Work?

Election of Delegates:

- **Voting:** Network users vote to elect delegates, also known as witnesses or block producers. The number of delegates can vary according to the protocol of a blockchain but typically ranges 20 to 100.
- **Voting Power:** Voting power is proportional to the number of tokens a user stakes, meaning that users holding more tokens will have a greater influence in the election process.

Validation and Block Production:

- **Rotation:** Elected delegates validate transactions and produce new blocks by taking turns. This rotation ensures that block production is distributed among all elected delegates.

- **Rewards:** Delegates receive transaction fees and, in some cases, additional token rewards.

Security and Accountability:

- **Accountability:** Delegates are accountable to the stakeholders who elected them. If a delegate fails to perform its duties or acts maliciously, it can be voted out and replaced by another candidate.
- **Incentives:** This accountability mechanism incentivizes delegates to operate in the best interest of the network.

Advantages of DPoS

- **Efficiency:** Transactions are processed faster, and throughput is higher compared to traditional PoW and PoS mechanisms due to the smaller number of block producers.
- Democratic Governance: The voting system introduces a more democratic approach to blockchain governance, allowing stakeholders to influence directly who validates transactions.
- Scalability: With fewer validators, reaching consensus is easier, enhancing the network's scalability.

Criticisms of DPoS

- **Centralization Risks:** With only a limited number of delegates responsible for verifying transactions, there is a risk of centralization. If a small, influential group gains control, it could undermine the decentralized nature of the blockchain.

- Voter Influence: Large holders of staked tokens have more voting power, leading to an unequal distribution of influence. "Whale" voters can disproportionately impact the election of delegates.
- Security Concerns: Fewer participants maintaining the network can make it easier for a 51% attack to be organized. Ensuring security requires robust measures and vigilant monitoring.

Examples of DPoS Blockchains

- **EOS:** Created by Dan Larimer, EOS was the first blockchain to implement DPoS. It is a scalable and user-friendly platform for dApps.
- TRON (TRX): TRON aims to create a decentralized internet and uses DPoS for its high transaction throughput and scalability.
- Lisk (LSK): Lisk is a blockchain application platform designed to make it easy for JavaScript developers to deploy sidechains and dApps. It uses DPoS for efficient and secure block production.

Delegated Proof of Stake introduces a more democratic and efficient approach to blockchain consensus mechanisms. By allowing stakeholders to elect delegates, DPoS enhances scalability and transaction throughput. However, it also presents risks such as centralization and unequal voter influence. As blockchain technology evolves, DPoS remains a significant innovation balancing efficiency and democratic governance.

Chapter 8

Proof of History (PoH)

Proof of History (PoH) is a novel consensus mechanism developed by Solana to address the timestamp problem in blockchain systems. It introduces a decentralized clock to timestamp transactions in a verifiable manner, eliminating the need for trusted timestamps.

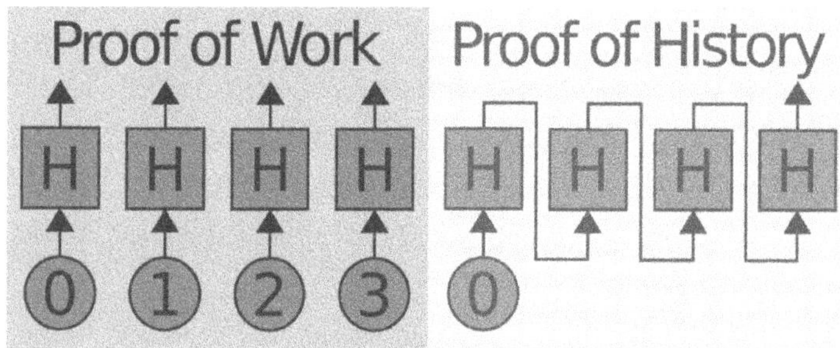

Source: Licdn

Understanding the Timestamp Problem

In decentralized systems, establishing the chronological order of transactions is crucial. Traditional methods involve nodes verifying timestamps, which can be slow and inefficient, requiring consensus from all nodes. PoH solves this by creating a cryptographic proof that time has passed between events, much like a centralized clock that all nodes can trust, ensuring proper transaction order.

PoH Works

Sequential Hashing:

- PoH uses a Verifiable Delay Function (VDF) to produce a series of proofs through a hash chain. Each hash represents a moment in time, serving as a timestamp for transactions.
- **Hash Stamping:** Transactions are stamped with a hash, indicating when they occurred. Other nodes can verify the transaction timing without relying on timestamps from other nodes.
- **Validator Clocks:** Each PoH validator has its clock, encoding the passage of time into the blockchain through the VDF. This reduces the need for heavy communication between validators to establish transaction times.

Advantages of PoH

- **Efficiency:** PoH provides reliable timestamping, leading to faster block production and validation, reducing delays, and boosting throughput.
- **Reduced Communication Overhead:** Validators do not need to continuously verify timestamps with each other, streamlining the consensus process.
- **Higher Confidence in Transaction Ordering:** Cryptographic proofs improve the precision and dependability of transaction ordering.

Comparisons to Traditional Blockchains

Traditional blockchains, such as those using Proof of Work (PoW), rely on strict block production order, often delayed by the need for network-wide confirmation. PoH allows block producers to independently verify time passage using the VDF, increasing speed and efficiency.

Challenges and Criticisms of PoH

- **Hardware Requirements:** PoH validators need specialized hardware, creating an entry barrier for potential participants, as documented in Solana's validator requirements.
- **Centralization Concerns:** PoH's efficiency gains come with centralization risks. Solana is considered more centralized compared to competitors like Ethereum.
- **Validator Centralization:** High hardware requirements and resource needs can reduce the number of validators, concentrating power and reducing decentralization.

Applications of PoH

- **Decentralized Finance (DeFi):** PoH is used to build scalable, efficient DeFi platforms, ensuring faster transaction processing and reliable timestamping.
- **Non-Fungible Tokens (NFTs):** PoH-based blockchains, like Solana, are used in NFT marketplaces for swift and verifiable transactions.
- **Gaming:** PoH's speed and efficiency make it suitable for blockchain gaming, where timely transactions are essential.

Proof of History (PoH) addresses the timestamp problem in blockchain technology by providing verifiable time-ordering of transactions using a VDF and sequential hashing. While it offers significant advantages in speed and efficiency, PoH also faces challenges related to hardware requirements and centralization. As blockchain technology evolves, PoH represents a critical development in improving the scalability and usability of decentralized networks.

Part 3
TOKENOMICS

Chapter 9

Deep Dive

Tokenomics, also often referred to as "token economics" investigates the underlying economics of cryptocurrencies. It studies the functionality, mechanisms, distribution, and long-term value factors of tokens. Tokenomics helps in ascertaining what gives the value to a cryptocurrency through isolating the token from its protocol. Here are the key concepts in tokenomics simplified:

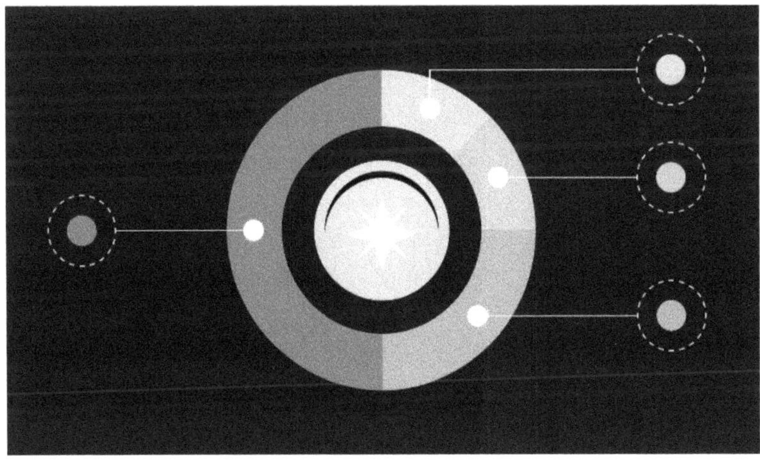

Source: Coinbase

1. Supply Dynamics

Circulating Supply: The current number of tokens available for trading in the market.

Maximum Supply: The total number of tokens that will ever exist.

Total Supply: The overall quantity of tokens minted or created, excluding those not yet circulated and burned.

Inflation and Deflation: Inflation refers to the increase in token supply over time, potentially affecting valuation by lowering prices if demand does not match. Deflation, on the other hand, involves a decrease in token supply, often through burning, which increases value due to scarcity.

2. Market Capitalization (Market Cap)

Market Cap: Calculated by multiplying the circulating supply by the token price, representing the total dollar value of all tokens in existence. Market cap is considered a better measure of value compared to price alone.

If crypto X has a circulating supply of 600,000 tokens and each token is valued at $2, its market cap is $1,200,000. If crypto Y has 100,000 tokens in circulation and each is valued at $3, its market cap is $300,000. So, while the individual $ price of crypto Y is higher, crypto X has a market cap that is four times as valuable.

Fully Diluted Value (FDV): The market capitalization if all possible tokens were in circulation, calculated by multiplying the current price by the maximum supply. It helps show potential future supply inflation.

3. Token Distribution

Fair Launch: Community mining without pre-allocated tokens for insiders, as seen with Bitcoin.

Pre-mine: Allocation of tokens to insiders and early investors before public launch, potentially risky if a large portion is allocated to a small group.

Private and Public Sales:

Private Sale: Early investors buy tokens at a discount, which may lead to selling pressure when their tokens unlock.

Public Sale: Tokens sold to the general public through ICOs, IEOs, or IDOs.

4. Vesting & Emissions Schedules

Vesting Schedule: A lock-up period for tokens before they can be sold, preventing sudden market dumps and stabilizing token prices.

Emissions: The rate at which new tokens are created and released. For example, Bitcoin's block rewards halve approximately every four years, reducing its emission rate.

5. Utility

Use-Case: Tokens serve specific purposes, such as paying protocol fees, staking for rewards, or participating in governance.

Revenue & Rewards: Some tokens generate revenue through staking, mining, or revenue-sharing mechanisms, driving demand and value.

6. Governance

Governance Tokens: These tokens enable voting on protocol changes and provide holders with influence over project decisions, distributed across the community for decision-making.

7. veTokenomics (Vote Escrowed Tokenomics)

Lock-Up Mechanism: Tokens are locked for a defined period, with longer locks increasing voting power. This encourages long-term commitment and reduces the risk of voting manipulation by large holders (whales).

Understanding a cryptocurrency's tokenomics involves considering supply dynamics, market capitalization, token distribution, vesting schedules, utility, governance, and innovative models like veTokenomics. These factors are crucial for assessing the current and future potential of a cryptocurrency and aiding investors in making informed decisions.

Rug Pulls

Rug pulls are a significant risk in the cryptocurrency space, particularly in DeFi and NFTs. This scam occurs when developers launch a project, sell their tokens, and then abandon the project, leaving investors with empty promises and depleted funds.

Types of Rug Pulls

Classic Rug Pull: Developers create a seemingly promising project, attract investors, and then swiftly sell off a large portion of the held tokens, crashing the token price and leaving investors with little to no value.

Slow Rug: Developers gradually exit a project, with communication dwindling, updates becoming scarce, and ultimately, the team abandoning the project. This may stem from overambitious goals or lack of expertise.

Identifying Unruggable Tokens

Unruggable tokens are deemed as such if they meet the following criteria:

Low Team-Held Tokens: Tokens are distributed fairly, with the team holding a minimal amount, reducing the risk of a sudden sell-off.

Renounced Ownership: The development team relinquishes ownership of the token contract, preventing them from making modifications or performing actions that could lead to a rug pull.

How to Avoid Rug Pulls?

1. **Research the Team:** Investigate the developers and their background. Projects with anonymous or unverified teams pose higher risks.

2. **Check Tokenomics:** Analyze how tokens are distributed. Projects where the team or early investors hold a significant portion of tokens are riskier.

3. **Look for Audits:** Ensure smart contracts are audited by reputable third parties to identify vulnerabilities or malicious code.

4. **Community Engagement:** Actively engaged and transparent communities are indicative of a reliable project less likely to be abandoned.

5. **Liquidity Locking:** Verify that liquidity is locked in a smart contract for a set period, preventing developers

from withdrawing liquidity and abandoning the project.

6. **Gradual Vesting:** Ensure there is a vesting schedule for team and advisor tokens, gradually releasing tokens over time to mitigate the risk of a sudden sell-off.

While rug pulls are unfortunately prevalent in the cryptocurrency and NFT space, recognizing warning signs and conducting thorough research can mitigate risks. It's crucial to identify and avoid untrusted projects, examine token distribution methods, and rely on community openness and third-party audits.

Part 4

BASICS 101: INVESTING IN CRYPTOCURRENCIES

Chapter 10

Let's Buy Cryptocurrencies

Now that you've learned the basics of cryptocurrencies, along with their risks and rewards, and determined that the sector is the right fit for you, it's time to start shopping for cryptos! As you know, almost all crypto transactions, investments, and trading take place online - after all, we're dealing with digital assets here. While there are ways to buy digital currencies using cash, such transactions are very rare. However, if you happen to know someone who has made a lot of money through cryptocurrencies and is willing to sell part of their holdings, you could buy cryptocurrencies directly from them by exchanging cash.

The most common way to purchase cryptocurrencies is through online cryptocurrency exchanges. Decentralized exchanges are an option that allows you to transact without the intervention of third parties. However, the method you choose may vary depending on your investment goals. For example, if you're a day trader, you may prefer the convenience of using traditional cryptocurrency broker services. But if your plan is simply to buy some cryptocurrencies and hold onto them, a reputable online or local exchange will suffice. In this chapter, we'll discuss the various types of exchanges, brokers, and other cryptocurrency service providers to help you choose the best options for your investment goals.

In This Chapter:

- Different avenues to buy cryptocurrencies
- Understanding the wide variety of crypto exchanges
- Understanding the role of Cryptocurrency Brokers
- Alternative ways to buy Cryptocurrencies

Finding the right method to purchase these highly in-demand digital assets may take some time and consideration. With changing regulations, increasing adoption rates, and growing market confidence in cryptocurrencies, it might be worth the effort. Whichever method of buying cryptocurrencies you choose, make sure you have a cryptocurrency wallet to securely hold your digital assets.

Steps in Buying Cryptocurrency:

1. Opt for a Reliable Platform: Choose a cryptocurrency exchange, broker, or ATM operating within your country. Read reviews, check their reputation, and review their security measures.

2. Choose a Payment Method: Most exchanges allow you to buy cryptocurrencies with fiat currencies such as USD. Link your bank account or other payment options to the exchange for smooth transactions.

3. Prepare for Identity Verification: Be ready to undergo identity verification or KYC procedures, which may include providing identification materials such as driver's licenses or social security cards.

4. Understand Transaction Fees: Familiarize yourself with the transaction fees associated with your chosen payment method and the exchange's fee policy.

5. Choose the Cryptocurrency: Research and analyze different cryptocurrencies to find one that aligns with your investment goals and risk appetite.

6. Set Your Investment Parameters: Determine the price and volume of the cryptocurrency you want to purchase. Utilize technical analysis techniques to make informed decisions and understand market trends.

7. Use Buy Limits: Take advantage of buy limits offered by exchanges and brokers to purchase investments at the best price. Define the maximum price you're willing to pay for the cryptocurrency and maintain control over your investments.

Chapter 11

CEX Vs DEX

A cryptocurrency exchange, also known as a digital currency exchange (DCE), is a web service that facilitates cash exchange for cryptocurrencies and vice versa. These exchanges are pivotal for converting fiat currencies into digital assets and often provide services to swap one cryptocurrency for another, such as Bitcoin to Ethereum or Dogecoin.

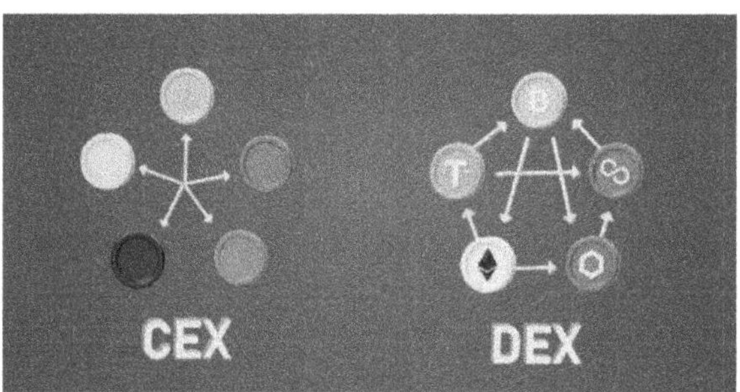

Comparing Brokers, Exchanges, and Wallets

When it comes to trading stocks, the decision of where to make a purchase is usually straightforward. It often involves online brokers, which grant access to major stock exchanges like the NYSE or NASDAQ. Brokers act as intermediaries, facilitating the buying and selling of financial assets.

However, the world of cryptocurrencies offers investors more alternatives. Instead of relying on brokers for intermediary services, cryptocurrency exchanges provide direct access to buying and selling digital assets. Here's a breakdown of the key differences and similarities:

Brokers and Exchanges: Brokers serve as intermediaries, while cryptocurrency exchanges offer a more diverse selection of digital assets. Exchanges may have higher transaction fees and are more vulnerable to cyberattacks, although many are constantly improving their security protocols.

Crypto Wallets: The best way to safeguard your cryptocurrency is by using a crypto wallet, a program designed to store your digital assets securely. Chapter 7 explores various types of cryptocurrency wallets and how to utilize them effectively.

Types of Cryptocurrency Exchanges:

- **Centralized Cryptocurrency Exchange (CEX):** These operate similarly to traditional stock exchanges, acting as intermediaries between buyers and sellers, and typically charge a commission for their services.
- **Decentralized Cryptocurrency Exchange (DEX):** Following the decentralized nature of cryptocurrencies, DEX operates without intermediaries.
- **Hybrid Cryptocurrency Exchange:** These combine features from both CEX and DEX to offer a blend of centralized and decentralized functionalities, aiming to provide the advantages of both.

Centralized Exchanges (CEXs):

Centralized exchanges operate much like traditional stock exchanges, bringing buyers and sellers together with the exchange acting as an intermediary. They typically charge a commission to process transactions. Here's an illustrative process on a centralized exchange:

1. Deposit your funds with the exchange.

2. The exchange holds your funds, similar to a bank.

3. Monitor the prices of available cryptocurrencies.

4. Trade your fiat currency (e.g., U. S. dollar) for cryptocurrencies (e.g., Bitcoin), or exchange one cryptocurrency for another.

5. Place your order.

6. The exchange matches your buy order with a seller, or vice versa.

Centralized exchanges usually support both crypto/crypto and fiat/crypto pairings:

Crypto/Crypto Pairing: Involves exchanging one cryptocurrency for another (e.g., Bitcoin for Ethereum).

Fiat/Crypto Pairing: Involves exchanging traditional currency for cryptocurrency (e.g., INR for Bitcoin).

One significant concern with centralized exchanges is hacking. While some exchanges have used their funds to reimburse customers post-hack, it's crucial to choose a centralized exchange with a robust financial situation and excellent security. With the increasing popularity of cryptocurrencies, more centralized exchanges will emerge, but it's essential to select a trustworthy one. Centralized exchanges are typically user-friendly, especially for beginners, and often offer customer support. For newcomers, starting with an exchange offering fiat/crypto pairings can be helpful.

Binance is a leading global cryptocurrency exchange platform that provides a wide range of digital asset trading and investment options. https://f7wx.short.gy/Binance

Bybit is a cryptocurrency exchange known for its robust derivatives trading platform and advanced trading features. https://f7wx.short.gy/Bybit

BingX is a cryptocurrency exchange offering spot, derivatives, and copy trading services with a focus on user-friendly and social trading experiences. https://bingx.pro/invite/RJGFZC

Gate.io is a comprehensive cryptocurrency exchange platform providing a wide array of digital asset trading options, including spot, margin, and futures trading. https://f7wx.short.gy/Gate.io

CoinDCX is a leading cryptocurrency exchange in India offering a wide range of digital asset trading and investment services. https://join.coindcx.com/invite/Ncsg

CoinSwitch is a prominent Indian cryptocurrency exchange and aggregator platform that simplifies trading across multiple exchanges. https://coinswitch.co/in/refer?tag=Swhmj

Decentralized Exchange (DEX)

A DEX allows trading to take place directly between peers without a central third party. In contrast to centralized exchanges, where customers' funds are held by a third party, DEXs enable peer-to-peer transactions using smart contracts and atomic swaps.

Smart Contracts: These are self-executing contracts that enforce the terms of the agreement between buyers and sellers. They are coded directly into the blockchain.

Advantages of DEXs:

- Decentralization: This aligns with the essence of cryptocurrencies, allowing users to control their assets without external third-party influence.
- Security: Since DEXs do not have a central exchange, they are harder to hack compared to centralized exchanges.

Potential Problems with DEXs:

Despite their advantages, DEXs have their fair share of problems:

- User Experience: Users can sometimes get locked out of their accounts if they forget their login information, and recovering lost data can be challenging.
- Low Liquidity: DEXs generally have less trading volume and liquidity than centralized exchanges, making high-volume trades problematic.
- Limited Fiat Support: Most DEXs do not support deposits and withdrawals in fiat currency, making them less accessible.

- High Costs and Slow Transactions: Transactions on DEXs can be costly and slow, with fees paid for several actions and delays due to block confirmations.

Popular Decentralized Exchanges:

Despite these challenges, some DEXs have become popular due to their traffic, liquidity, and trading volume:

Uniswap: A decentralized trading protocol that enables automated liquidity provision and the trading of any ERC-20 token on Ethereum.

SushiSwap: A simple Automated Market Maker (AMM) decentralized exchange that allows users to swap various tokens.

Balancer: A tool that lets people put their portfolio assets to work in different ways.

1inch: A decentralized exchange aggregator that sources liquidity and provides users with the best possible trading rates.

Although DEXs often face issues like low liquidity and limited fiat support, they remain relatively secure and play a crucial role in the cryptocurrency ecosystem. Continuous developments and improvements in the decentralized finance space ensure that DEXs will continue to be important in the future.

What is Liquidity Mining?

Liquidity mining allows cryptocurrency holders to maximize earnings by providing liquidity to decentralized finance (DeFi) platforms. Users deposit their tokens into liquidity pools to earn rewards, which may come in the form of additional tokens or a share of transaction fees.

APY: Annual Percentage Yield is the potential annual return that one can achieve from liquidity mining. Some liquidity pools offer very high APYs, often exceeding 100%, allowing users to grow their holdings much faster.

Understanding Impermanent Loss

Impermanent loss occurs when the value of tokens in a liquidity pool diverges from the value of the same tokens held independently. It is termed "impermanent" because this loss is not permanent and arises due to price fluctuations of tokens in the pool. Impermanent loss is more common with volatile cryptocurrencies but can affect any liquidity pool.

Risk vs. Reward: While liquidity mining can be lucrative, impermanent loss happens when the value of the pools tokens deviates significantly. However, high-risk cryptocurrencies often offer higher returns.

Choosing a Liquidity Pool

When selecting a liquidity pool for mining, consider factors such as risk tolerance and token fundamentals:

- Risk Management: Assess the risk associated with each liquidity pool and select cryptocurrencies that align with your level of risk tolerance.
- Fundamentals: Choose tokens with strong fundamentals and a clear use case to minimize impermanent loss.
- Education: Enhance your understanding of risk tolerance and asset selection by utilizing educational resources.

Now, whether you're a new or experienced investor, selecting the right cryptocurrency exchange is crucial. Here are some tips to help you choose the best exchange for your needs:

Security

- **Research:** Prioritize exchanges with a proven track record of security and reliability.
- **Authentication:** Choose exchanges that offer two-factor or multi-factor authentication.
- **Cold Storage:** Look for exchanges that store the majority of funds offline in cold storage.
- **Proof of Reserve:** Select exchanges that conduct regular audits of their reserves to ensure transparency and trustworthiness.

Supported Currencies

- **Cryptocurrency Availability:** Ensure the exchange supports the cryptocurrencies you plan to trade or invest in.
- **Fiat Support:** If you plan to buy crypto with fiat currency, select an exchange that supports fiat-to-crypto transactions.

Liquidity

- **Trading Volume:** Check the liquidity of the exchange and its trading volume to ensure you can carry out fast and efficient transactions.
- **Market Depth:** Deeper markets allow you to buy and sell assets without significantly affecting their prices.

Fees

- **Transaction Fees:** Compare the fee structures of various exchanges, including trading volume discounts and bid-ask spreads.
- **Security before Fees:** Prioritize security and reliability over low fees to protect your investment.

Ease of Use

- **User Interface:** Choose user-friendly exchanges with intuitive interface designs, especially if you are a beginner.
- **Mobile Support:** Select exchanges with mobile app support for convenient trading on the go.

Location

- **Regulatory Compliance:** Be aware of the regulatory environment in the exchange's location to understand its impact on your trading activities.
- **Local vs. International Exchanges:** Consider whether the exchange accepts local fiat currencies and the fees for domestic users.

Method of Payment

- **Payment Options:** Choose exchanges with convenient payment methods, such as bank transfers, PayPal, or credit/debit cards.
- **Consider the Fees:** Keep in mind that more convenient options usually come with higher fees.

Customer Support

- **Responsive Customer Support:** Opt for exchanges with responsive customer support to address any issues promptly.
- **Avoid Account Lockouts:** Review customer feedback and forums to avoid exchanges with a poor history of customer support and account lockouts.

Trading Features

- **Advanced Trading Features:** For active traders, select exchanges that offer advanced trading options like margin trading and various order types.
- **Understand the Risk:** Ensure you understand the risks associated with these advanced features before using them.

Transaction Limits

- **Daily Limits:** Check the transaction limits on the exchange, especially if you have specific trading or investment targets.
- **Check Limits:** Verify the transaction limits on the exchange's website before creating an account.

By carefully considering these factors, you can select a cryptocurrency exchange that aligns with your investment objectives, risk tolerance, and trading preferences. Remember to prioritize security, liquidity, and reliability to safeguard your assets in the volatile cryptocurrency market.

Do This

- Open a cryptocurreny CEX account to start investing in cryptocurrency.
  - Pick a reliable platform and dive into investments. You can do this online, through platforms such as Binance, Bybit, CoinDCX and more.

- Decide your asset-allocation strategy.
  - Decide how much you will invest in cryptocurrencies.
  - Within cryptos, decide how much risk you're willing to take.
    - How much in largr-cap cryptos?
    - How much in each sectors?
    - How much in meme coins?

- Automate your investments.
  - Create a separate account to park your savings (to Invest!). Set up auto-transfers from your salary account to your investment accounts.
  - Start systematic investment plans (SIPs) – they're great to balance out market volatility.

Chapter 12

Cryptocurrency Wallets

Cryptocurrency wallets are tools that store digital money. Unlike conventional wallets used to store credit and debit cards, cryptocurrency wallets store the private and public keys necessary for their proper function. Cryptocurrencies rely on these wallets for sending, receiving, and securely storing digital money.

Importance of Cryptocurrency Wallets

Cryptocurrency wallets are crucial for the effective use of digital currencies. While Bitcoin and other digital currencies are decentralized in theory, their functionality relies on individual miners and nodes. The blockchain, which records transactions, is distributed across the network. Miners hold pieces of the blockchain on their devices, but the entire blockchain is dispersed across the network. Cryptocurrency wallets facilitate transactions and ensure the integrity of this decentralized system by storing private and public keys.

Private keys act as passwords for accessing wallet addresses, while public keys enable the receipt of cryptocurrencies. When someone transfers cryptocurrency to you, they transfer ownership to your wallet address, and this transaction is recorded on the blockchain. The unique wallet address serves as your identifier, ensuring secure transactions.

Key Terms

Before delving deeper into cryptocurrency wallets, it is important to understand some key terms:

- **Hot Wallet:** A hot wallet is connected to the internet and is convenient for frequent transactions. However, it is more vulnerable to hacking compared to a cold wallet.
- **Cold Wallet:** A cold wallet is not connected to the internet and is more secure for storing significant amounts of cryptocurrencies. It is less susceptible to hacking attacks.
- **Wallet Address:** A wallet address is a string of characters used for sending and receiving cryptocurrencies. It is similar to an email address but is specific to cryptocurrency transactions. Each wallet address is unique to a particular wallet.
- **Public Key:** A public key is a cryptographic code that allows you to receive cryptocurrencies into your account. It is mathematically linked to your wallet address but is not the same as it. You can share your public key with others to receive cryptocurrencies.
- **Private Key:** A private key is a secure code linked to the public key used in encryption and decryption processes. It functions as a password to access and manage the cryptocurrencies in your wallet. The private key must be kept secure and confidential to ensure the safety of your funds.

By understanding these terms and the functionality of cryptocurrency wallets, you can securely manage and utilize your digital assets.

Private Keys Example: 03bf350d2821375158a608b51e3e898 e507fe47f2d2e8c774de4a9a7edecf74eda.

Public Key Example: 99b1ebcfc11a13df5161aba8160460fe1601d541.

How Wallets and Keys Work Together

Cryptocurrency wallets do not store the cryptocurrencies themselves; they store the owner's public and private keys, which control access to the digital assets. When someone sends you cryptocurrency, they are essentially transferring ownership to your wallet address. To own these coins, your private key must match the public key in the transaction. The blockchain verifies this match, ensuring the validity of the transaction.

Public and Private Keys

- **Public Key:** Similar to an account number, the public key is shared openly and used to receive funds. It is derived from the private key.
- **Private Key:** Comparable to a password, the private key must remain secret. It grants access to the funds associated with the corresponding public key.

Wallet Addresses

- **Unique Addresses:** Wallet addresses are unique identifiers derived from public keys. This ensures funds are sent to the correct recipient.

- **Address Generation:** Users can generate multiple wallet addresses without limitation, providing flexibility and security.

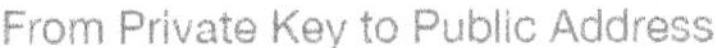

Source: Bitlra

Security of Wallets

Wallets are generally secure, but they can be vulnerable to malware. For instance, malware can intercept and alter wallet addresses copied to the clipboard, leading to funds being sent to an unintended address. Always double-check wallet addresses before confirming transactions.

Example Wallet Address

An example of a Bitcoin wallet address, often associated with Satoshi Nakamoto, the creator of Bitcoin, is:

1A1zP1eP5QGefi2DMPTfTL5SLmv7DivfNa

This address consists of a mix of numbers and letters in both upper and lower case.

Storing Wallet Keys

Importance of Security

- **Private Keys:** Keeping private keys secure is crucial. Without them, you cannot access your funds, and if they are lost, recovery is impossible.
- **Storage Methods:**
    - **Cold Storage Wallets:** These physical devices are not connected to the Internet, providing high security.
    - **Hot Storage Wallets:** These are connected to the Internet, offering convenience but higher risk.

Seed Phrases

Seed phrases are another security measure. They are typically 12-24 word sequences used to recover private keys and access wallets. They must be stored securely, similar to private keys.

Key Points

- **Decentralization:** Your funds are not stored or controlled by any central authority.
- **Transparency and Anonymity:** Transactions are transparent on the blockchain, but private keys remain anonymous.
- **Irretrievability:** If you lose your private keys or seed phrases, access to your funds is permanently lost.

What Happens if You Lose Your Private Keys?

Losing your private key means losing access to your funds permanently. This irretrievability underscores the importance of secure storage.

Can You Change Your Private Key?

Private keys cannot be changed once created. If you need a new private key, you must create a new wallet account. Ensuring the secure storage of your private key eliminates the need for changing it.

Self-Custody and Crypto Wallets

Self-custody of your cryptocurrency means transferring your assets from a centralized exchange to your control, where you own the private key. If you have the private key, you have full control over the assets in the wallet.

Centralized vs. Self-Custody

- **Centralized Custody:** When you store your cryptocurrency on platforms like Binance or Coinbase, they hold all the private keys to your coins, meaning they control your assets.
- **Self-Custody:** By moving your cryptocurrency to a self-custody wallet, you hold the private keys and have full control and responsibility over your assets.

The Responsibility of Self-Custody

In self-custody, if you lose your wallet password, no central authority can reset it for you. The only way to access your wallet again is through your seed phrase.

What is a Seed Phrase?

When you create a new wallet, the wallet provider generates a seed phrase for you. This is a random series of 12-24 words that serves as the key to your crypto funds.

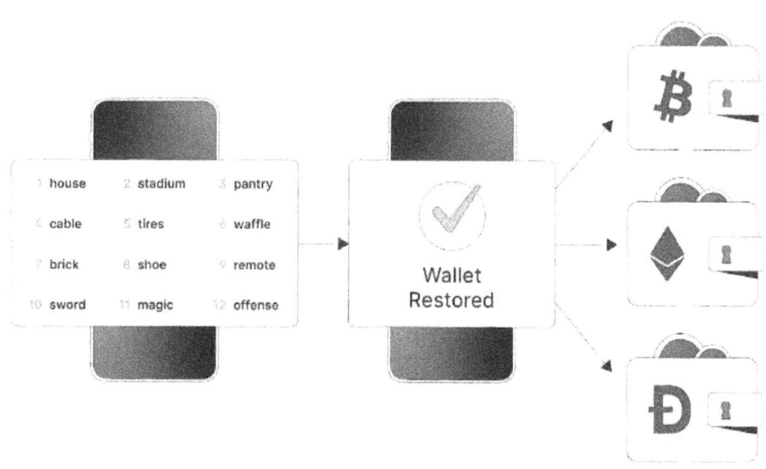

Source: Medium

Example Seed Phrase: all tourist alarm travel crew logic random sight bulb ritual frozen help

Importance of Seed Phrases

- **Ease of Use:** Seed phrases are easier to remember and enter than long alphanumeric strings.
- **Security:** If you lose your seed phrase, you lose access to your funds forever. Keeping your seed phrase secure is crucial for keeping your crypto secure.

Best Practices

- **Write it down:** Write your seed phrase and store copies in multiple places.
- **Engrave it:** Some people engrave their seed phrase on durable materials like metal.
- **Store securely:** Keep your seed phrase where no one else can access it, such as in a safe.

BIP39 and Seed Phrase Security

In 2013, the Bitcoin Improvement Proposal 39 (BIP39) introduced the standard for seed phrases, which are a list of 2048 words used to derive private keys.

- **Security:** A 12-word seed phrase provides 128 bits of security due to the 2^{128} possible combinations. This level of security makes it nearly impossible for even the most experienced hacker to guess your phrase.
- **Longer Phrases:** A longer phrase, such as 24 words, increases security exponentially.

Self-custody of your cryptocurrency involves moving your assets from a centralized exchange to a wallet where you control the private keys. The seed phrase is crucial for recovering your wallet if you lose your password or device. The security of the seed phrase is paramount to protecting your crypto assets. Securing your digital wealth is possible only if you know and practice the best ways to store and manage your seed phrase.

Types of Cryptocurrency wallets

Understanding the different types of cryptocurrency wallets is fundamental to managing and securing your digital assets. Here are five of the most popular types of cryptocurrency wallets, sorted by their safety levels, from least safe to most safe:

1. Online Wallet

Definition: Online wallets, or web wallets, allow users to access their cryptocurrencies through the internet. The private keys are stored on the wallet provider's server, and funds can be accessed from various devices such as mobile phones, tablets, and computers.

Pros:

- Transactions are carried out quickly.
- Supports multiple cryptocurrencies.
- Ideal for active trading and convenient on-the-go usage.
- **Cons:**
- High exposure to potential hacking or fraud.
- Susceptible to computer viruses.
- Private keys are stored by a third party.

Examples:

Binance.us: Secure and regulated, with high security for experienced users.

Coinbase: User-friendly, supports over 170 digital assets, multi-signature, and two-factor authentication.

MetaMask: A decentralized wallet popular for Ethereum and NFTs on numerous network blockchains.

2. **Mobile Wallet**

Definition: Mobile wallets are applications on cell phones used to store and use cryptocurrencies for transactions, often in physical stores where crypto payments are accepted.

Pros:

- More secure than online wallets.
- Convenient for on-the-go usage.
- Supports features such as scanning QR codes.

Cons:

- Risk of losing stored funds if the phone is lost or damaged without a seed phrase backup.
- Susceptible to mobile viruses or malware.

Examples:

Trust Wallet: User-friendly mobile app supporting over 160,000 coins and tokens, popular for NFTs and dApps.

3. **Desktop Wallet**

Definition: Desktop wallets are software programs installed on your computer. They are more secure if the computer remains disconnected from the internet, thus functioning as a cold wallet.

Pros:

- Convenient for trading cryptos from a computer.
- Private keys are not stored on a third-party server.
- Safer than online wallets when offline.

Cons:

- Not convenient for on-the-go use.
- Security decreases when connected to the internet.
- Risk of data loss if the computer fails without a backup.

Setup Note: Download the wallet on an internet-connected computer, transfer the latest version to the offline computer via USB.

4. Hardware Wallet

Definition: Hardware wallets store private keys on a hardware device similar to a USB stick. They are typically used offline, hence referred to as cold wallets.

Source: Ledger

Pros:

- Among the highest security wallets in crypto.
- Ideal for holding large amounts of cryptocurrency not used daily.

Cons:

- Expensive.
- Not very user-friendly for beginners.

Examples:

Ledger Nano S: Popular, highly rated, and links to Ledger Live for easy asset monitoring.

Trezor: High-security hardware wallet from SatoshiLabs, links with the Trezor Suite app for mobile phones.

5. Paper Wallet

Definition: Paper wallets are physical printouts of your public and private keys on a piece of paper, serving as extremely secure cold storage.

Source: Blockgeeks

Pros:

- Ultra hacker-proof.
- Not stored on any digital device or third-party server.

Cons:

- Not user-friendly for non-technical users.
- Difficult to use for daily transactions.
- Physical risks such as damage or loss by fire.

Setup Note: Use generators like bitaddress.org or Bitcoin.com to create a paper wallet.

> *"Each type of cryptocurrency wallet has its pros*
> *and cons, and the best choice depends on your*
> *needs and risk tolerance. Online and mobile*

wallets offer convenience and ease of use, while desktop, hardware, and paper wallets provide higher levels of security for long-term storage. Always ensure you secure your seed phrases and private keys to protect your digital assets effectively."

Choosing a Crypto Wallet

Choosing the right type of cryptocurrency wallet depends on the security level you require, the type of cryptocurrencies you hold, how often you make transactions, and your desired level of anonymity. Here are some key considerations to help you choose the right wallet for your needs:

Security

Cold Storage for Large Reserves:

- **Recommendation:** Use highly secure cold storage for significant cryptocurrency reserves.
- **Cost:** Ensure the cost of the hardware wallet is justified by the value of your crypto holdings.
- **Authentication:** Consider the type of authentication required by the wallet.
- **Website Security:** Check the security of the wallet provider's website.
- **Reviews:** Look at reviews on sites like CoinCentral. com, 99Bitcoins.com, and CryptoCompare.com to form an educated opinion.

Hot Wallets for Active Trading:

- Use online or mobile wallets for small and irregular amounts.

- Understand that there is an added security risk compared to cold wallets.

Crypto Ownership

Single Cryptocurrency Wallets:

Use Case: If you hold only one type of cryptocurrency.

Examples:

Bitcoin: Bitcoin Core Wallet, Mycelium, Electrum.

Ethereum: Ethereum Wallet, MetaMask, MyEtherWallet.

Multicurrency Wallets:

Use Case: If you hold multiple cryptocurrencies.

Examples:

MetaMask: A mobile wallet app supporting over 200 types of digital tokens.

Exodus: A desktop wallet app that stores private keys on your device.

Transaction Fees

High transaction costs can eat into your profits, especially if you are an active trader. Assess the transaction fees charged by the wallet and match them with your trading or spending behavior.

Anonymity

Anonymous Wallets: Add an extra layer of security by dissociating personal information from funds.

Examples:

BitLox: A hardware wallet ensuring security and anonymity.

Electrum: A trusted desktop wallet.

Samourai: A mobile wallet focused on privacy and security.

Securing Your Wallet

Backup:

- Regularly back up your cryptocurrency wallets to protect against data loss.
- Store backups in a safe location, separate from your primary wallet.
- Include PIN codes, usernames, and passwords in your backup plan.

Multiple Wallets:

- Diversify by using multiple wallets to spread risk.
- Combine hardware wallets for large amounts with smaller amounts in mobile, desktop, or online wallets.

Additional Security Features:

- **Two-Factor Authentication (2FA):** Use apps like Google Authenticator for an additional layer of security.
- **Encryption:** Encrypt your wallet to add a password for withdrawals and encrypt your backups.
- **Strong Passwords:** Use long, complex passwords with a combination of letters, numbers, and symbols.
- **Software Updates:** Keep your wallet software up to date to incorporate the latest security fixes.

Remember Your Hiding Spot:

If you hide your wallets or backups, choose a memorable and secure location to avoid losing access to your funds.

113

Keep a watch:

Here are some cryptocurrencies to watch out for in the L1 sector:

1. Solana - $SOL

2. Ton Blockchain - $TON

3. Kaspa Currency - $KAS

4. Injective Protocol - $INJ

Not financial advice, but these are just my personal favorites and are for learning purposes.

Chapter 13

Types of Cryptocurrencies

You've probably heard of Bitcoin, the original cryptocurrency. However, there are many other well-known and valuable cryptocurrencies available today. Some believe that Bitcoin may not be the best cryptocurrency to own or invest in, considering the improvements made by other digital coins to address its drawbacks.

Despite these concerns, Bitcoin holds value for several reasons. It is the only truly decentralized cryptocurrency, providing ultimate control over wealth and freedom from global governments. As the category king, it pioneered a new industry and is widely recognized, adding to its value. With only 21 million Bitcoins ever to be mined, of which 93% is already mined, its value could rise due to the law of supply and demand if it maintains its category king status. However, some investors avoid Bitcoin due to its high energy consumption, slow and costly transactions, and lack of real utility. As of this writing, Bitcoin and Ethereum ETFs had been approved by the SEC.

In this chapter, I discuss some of the most famous cryptocurrencies as of 2024. However, since the cryptocurrency market is constantly changing, I also provide guidance on navigating the ever-evolving landscape of upcoming cryptos for the years to come.

Coins, Altcoins, and Tokens

If you've read any crypto-related articles, you may have seen terms like coins, altcoins, and tokens used interchangeably. However, there are actual differences between them.

Coins

Coins are the native cryptocurrencies of the specific blockchain they run on. For example, Bitcoin is a coin because it runs on the Bitcoin blockchain. Since Bitcoin was the first-ever cryptocurrency, all other native blockchain coins are considered alternative coins. Therefore, in the world of cryptocurrency, "coin" primarily refers to Bitcoin.

Some also consider Ethereum a coin as it runs on its blockchain. As cryptocurrencies gained popularity in the 2010s, many other cryptocurrencies emerged from Bitcoin or Ethereum forks—splitting from the original blockchain. As blockchain technology becomes more mainstream, more novel blockchains are emerging.

Key Points:

- **Bitcoin:** The first and most recognized cryptocurrency, known for its decentralization and brand recognition.
- **Ethereum:** Often considered a coin, it runs on its blockchain and introduced smart contracts.

Altcoins

All other cryptocurrency coins, except Bitcoin (and for some, except Ethereum as well), which run on native or independent blockchains, are grouped under altcoins. Prominent examples include Litecoin, Dogecoin, and Binance Coin.

The first altcoin was Namecoin, created in April 2011. Namecoin is a decentralized open-source information registration and transfer system.

Examples:

- **Litecoin:** Created as a "lighter" version of Bitcoin with faster transaction times.
- **Dogecoin:** Started as a meme but gained significant popularity and a strong community.
- **Binance Coin:** Created as an ERC-20 token on the Ethereum blockchain, but now part of the Binance Chain.

Tokens

A token is a digital representation of an asset or utility, usually living on top of another blockchain instead of having its blockchain. This serves a different purpose than the monetary aspect expressed by coins and altcoins. Value extraction tokens can represent any tradable asset. Fungible means replaceable by an identical non-specific item. For example, you can exchange a $100 bill for five $20 bills or two $50 bills, making it fungible.

Tokens can represent all fungible and tradable assets, from commodities to loyalty points and cryptocurrencies. You can even tokenize real estate. To determine whether a cryptocurrency is a coin or a token, check if it has its blockchain. If it does, it is a coin. If it works with an existing blockchain, it's a token.

Examples:

- **Utility Tokens:** Used to access a service within a blockchain ecosystem (e.g., Basic Attention Token within the Brave browser).
- **Security Tokens:** Represent ownership interest in a real-world asset such as land.
- **Stablecoins:** Pegged to a stable asset such as the US dollar (e.g., USDT, USDC).

Criterion	Coins	Altcoins	Tokens
Definition	Native cryptocurrencies on their own blockchain (e.g., Bitcoin, Ethereum)	Cryptocurrencies that are alternatives to Bitcoin, often with unique features (e.g., Litecoin, Ripple)	Digital assets created on existing blockchains (e.g., ERC-20 tokens on Ethereum)
Blockchain	Have their own independent blockchain	Have their own independent blockchain	Operate on another cryptocurrency's blockchain
Creation	Created through mining (Proof of Work) or staking (Proof of Stake)	Created through mining or staking, often using modified or new protocols	Created through smart contracts on existing blockchains
Use Case	Primarily used as a digital currency for transactions, store of value, or investment	Similar to coins but often have additional features like smart contracts, privacy, etc.	Often represent assets, utility, or access rights within a specific platform or service
Examples	Bitcoin (BTC), Ethereum (ETH)	Litecoin (LTC), Monero (XMR), Cardano (ADA)	Chainlink (LINK), Uniswap (UNI), Tether (USDT)

Celebrating Celebrity Cryptocurrencies by Market Cap

One of the fastest ways to navigate popular cryptocurrencies is by checking their ranking based on market capitalization, or market cap. Traditionally, market cap represents the value of a company traded on the stock market, calculated by multiplying the total number of shares by the present share price.

In the crypto world, market capitalization reflects the value of all units of a specific cryptocurrency available for sale. To calculate a cryptocurrency's market cap, multiply its current price by its circulating supply—approximately the number of coins in circulation among the general public.

Market Cap = Price × Circulating Supply

Understanding a crypto's market cap and its ranking versus other coins provides insights into its popularity and potential profitability. You can find market cap data for all cryptocurrencies on websites like coinmarketcap.com, cryptocompare.com, coincodex.com, and coingecko.com.

However, market cap alone cannot determine a cryptocurrency's investment potential. Various factors such as forks, regulation, rumors, blockchain, community, utility, and mission influence a cryptocurrency's value. A higher market cap isn't always advantageous; risk-tolerant investors might prefer lower-cap cryptocurrencies for potential growth, while risk-averse individuals may opt for higher-cap coins to minimize volatility and risk of loss.

Bitcoin

Bitcoin (BTC), introduced in January 2009, was the first cryptocurrency. The genesis block of Bitcoin carries a message critiquing irresponsible policies of banks and governments, signaling Bitcoin's intent to challenge centralized authority.

Bitcoin as a Store of Value

Bitcoin's strongest case is its role as a "store of value that cannot be manipulated." Its decentralized network operates on thousands of computers globally, recording all transactions on the blockchain—a digital ledger distributed across the network. This decentralization ensures authenticity and legitimacy, making the network permissionless and censorship-resistant.

Token Release Schedule

Bitcoin's creator, Satoshi Nakamoto, limited its supply to 21 million coins, emphasizing verifiable scarcity—a fundamental aspect of Bitcoin's value proposition. Approximately 2.1 million bitcoins remain to be mined as of May 2024. Once the total supply is exhausted, miners' income will rely solely on transaction fees, reinforcing Bitcoin's scarcity and store of value narrative.

Mining Difficulty

'Mining difficulty' refers to the level of computational effort required to mine a Bitcoin block. This difficulty is dynamically adjusted by the Bitcoin network to maintain a consistent rate of new coin production. As computational power increases and more miners join

the network, the difficulty adjusts proportionally to ensure a steady issuance of new bitcoins.

As Satoshi Nakamoto put it: "As computers get faster and the total computing power applied to creating bitcoins increases, the difficulty increases proportionally to keep the total new production constant. Thus, it is known in advance how many new bitcoins will be created every year in the future."

Halving

Every four years, Bitcoin undergoes a halving event, where the block reward for miners is reduced by half. This periodic reduction in block reward is designed to slow down the rate of new coin issuance, ultimately leading to a gradual increase in Bitcoin's value. Once the maximum supply of 21 million bitcoins is reached, no more bitcoins will be created. This scarcity is expected to drive up the value of mined coins over time.

Bitcoin has a maximum supply of 21 million coins, and there will only be 32 halving events in total. After the 32nd halving event, which is expected to occur around the year 2140, the maximum supply of 21 million coins will have been reached.

During the current halving in 2024, the number of bitcoins released per block will decrease to around 3.125.

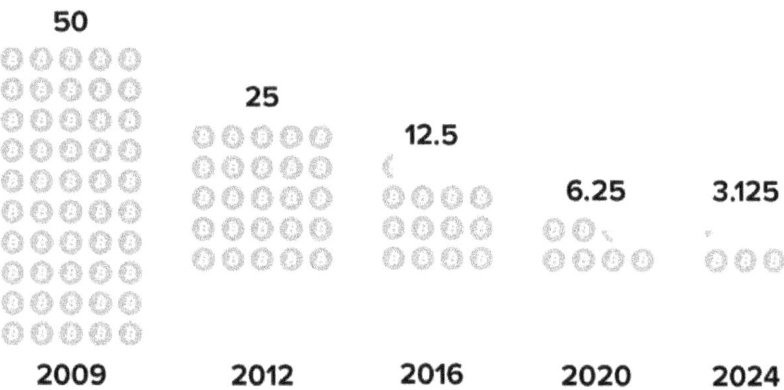

The anticipation of halving events has historically contributed to positive sentiment and price appreciation in the Bitcoin market. This phenomenon is driven by the expectation of reduced inflation and increased scarcity, aligning with Bitcoin's deflationary nature.

The Lightning Network

Bitcoin, originally conceived as a decentralized digital payment system, faced scalability challenges as its user base grew. Slow transaction speeds, high fees, and limited scalability hindered Bitcoin's ability to serve as a viable medium for everyday transactions.

In response to these challenges, the Lightning Network was developed as a second-layer solution to enhance Bitcoin's scaleability. Operating on an "off-chain" protocol, the Lightning Network enables fast and inexpensive transactions, complementing the main Bitcoin blockchain. Transactions conducted on the Lightning Network are nearly instantaneous and incur minimal fees, making them ideal for microtransactions and everyday use cases.

While the Bitcoin network processes around 7 transactions per second, the Lightning Network boasts the potential to handle up to 1,000,000 transactions per second theoretically. This scalability solution significantly improves Bitcoin's utility and usability as a digital currency.

It's worth noting that the Lightning Network is not exclusive to Bitcoin; other cryptocurrencies like Litecoin have also implemented similar solutions. Additionally, Ethereum and Solana have developed their own 'Layer 2' scaling solutions, aligning with the principles of the Lightning Network to enhance transaction throughput and scalability.

Ethereum

Ethereum, created by programmer Vitalik Buterin and launched in 2015, is an open-source, decentralized blockchain derivative. Think of it as a piece of land on which people erect homes, buildings, skyscrapers, and open businesses to be used by other people for trade. As more people come, more buildings are put up. The city becomes more bustling, like New York City.

In this analogy, Ethereum is the land, the users are the people, and decentralized apps are the businesses.

Ether (ETH) is the native token of Ethereum. It is the currency that powers every engagement in the city. It's used to pay for transactions and interact with services.

The Merge

Ethereum was originally secured using the Proof of Work (PoW) consensus mechanism, the same mechanism that secures Bitcoin, but on the 15th of September, 2022, it went through an upgrade that turned it into a Proof of Stake mechanism, a transition often referred to as 'The Merge'.

In simple terms, a consensus mechanism validates transactions and helps keep a network secure. PoW is highly energy-intensive and requires a lot of computational work, resulting in a significant environmental impact. On the other hand, PoS enables blockchains to operate more energy-efficiently while preserving decentralization. Each mechanism has its best qualities for various purposes.

With PoS, ETH holders stake their coins to validate transactions and create new blocks. In return, the network rewards these validators for processing transactions, and their stake is partially slashed if they act maliciously, ensuring honest behavior. At the heart of Ethereum's PoS system is the Beacon Chain, which used to be a separate entity from the main Ethereum network. The two were officially merged on the 15th of September, 2022.

Smart contracts and decentralized applications

Ethereum's value proposition is derived from its ability to enable developers to implement their decentralized applications (dApps) on the blockchain. Ethereum was the first-ever programmable blockchain, thus, incorporating the essence in allowing the advent of smart contracts. A smart contract is an on-chain agreement built into a network consisting of computer code that automatically executes a set of specified actions depending on the requirements it is given. For example, a smart contract can be designed to send 1 ETH to a specified address every 24 hours:

IF 24 hours have passed (the trigger), THEN send 1 ETH (the execution).

Smart contracts can be highly complicated and can enable many types of transactions. The Ethereum network acts like a computer with features called scripts, whose details and wallet balances are reflected in Ethereum's ledger. Once the conditions of a smart contract are met and agreed upon by all parties, the contract will do as it was supposed to do. A smart contract thus is on the blockchain, a sure way of ensuring no one changes the agreement of a smart contract, also known as \"Code is Law.\" If it is not in the smart contract code, then it will not happen, but if it is in the code, then it will happen.

Technology enforces the rules, and therefore an intermediary is not required, that is the basis of decentralized finance.

Of course, all these smart contracts carry risks. For example, if something goes wrong and the smart contract is not updatable after launching, then all the funds locked within it could be locked forever. Several smart contracts can be combined to develop decentralized applications. As we know, the innovations and versatility that Ethereum brought have resulted in the development of DeFi. On the Ethereum blockchain, one can access a wide plethora of decentralized applications, with use cases ranging from financial services (like Aave and Uniswap) to art and collectibles (like OpenSea). DApps are at the core of DeFi, offering endless possibilities for innovation and use cases.

The Ethereum Virtual Machine

The Ethereum Virtual Machine (EVM) is the computational engine and software platform that processes, wherein many people call it the heart of Ethereum. It executes smart contracts and computes each new block that is attached to the Ethereum blockchain. The EVM further allows the development and creation of dApps built on the Ethereum network.

'EVM-compatible networks' quite straightforwardly mean networks running an instance of EVM. Now, these networks can interoperate with Ethereum, offering most of the dApps and DeFi services found within the Ethereum ecosystem. The reason for this is that developers can launch their applications over any EVM chain with minimal modifications, given that the EVM is compatible. Lacking EVM compatibility, the developers would be forced to rewrite their entire code.

Ethereum dApps can also easily migrate to EVM-compatible networks.

Ethereum Gas fees

Gas fees refer to payments that a user makes during a transaction to remunerate validateurs for computation done. Ethereum (ETH) validators run computer software to verify transactions and add blocks to a blockchain. This process requires the usage of electricity, so the gas fee is paid to the validators as a reward to compensate the cost of the electricity used. There's also a portion of the fee that is burned and removed from circulation. The cost of gas in Ethereum is not a fixed number—it varies depending on the demand on the Ethereum network. The gas fee in Ethereum remains dynamic. When there's more demand, gas fees are higher.

Ethereum users can set a 'tip' to reduce the network gas fee for a given transaction. The tip is used to give a sense of priority to a transaction. The higher the tip assigned to a transaction, the likelier it is to be picked up by a validator sooner than one with a very minimal tip.

You can monitor gas prices using tools such as Etherscan https://etherscan.io/gastracker

What is Gwei?

Ethereum gas fees are what you must pay to use the blockchain. They are paid in the blockchain's native currency, ETH or ether. ETH gas fees are denoted in gwei, a denomination of ETH. One gwei equals 0.000000001 ETH or 1. So if your gas price costs 0.000000001, it costs 1 gwei.

What is the Maximal Extractable Value (MEV) of Ethereum's invisible tax?

MEV is an abbreviation of Miner Extractable Value, which is defined as the potential profit an Ethereum miner can make by reordering transactions within the produced blocks. This means getting a maximal payment since people generally pay high gas fees for transactions to be confirmed as fast as possible. Originally, MEV was part of the PoW mechanism with miners allowed to choose the transactions they wanted to include and change the correct ordering to profit from different strategies.

With Ethereum's transition to PoS in 2022, mining is out of the equation, but MEV isn't. Instead of miners, validators check whether the blocks are valid and gather MEV. MEV activity is grouped under what's termed 'searchers,' who generate superior software and bot codes to spot and maximize MEV opportunities. Once an opportunity is visible, he gathers a transaction bundle to be executed to extract the projected profit.

Top 50 major cryptocurrencies

You can slice your way through the top 50 major cryptocurrencies and still not find the one you want to enter into a long-term relationship with. At this point, it's exactly like online dating, but with cryptocurrencies that need to fit the bill in your portfolio. You will need to evaluate the first impression you get from each, make some small investments, and do further research to determine reality in deciding whether a particular currency is eligible to occupy a significant share of your cryptocurrency portfolio.

You can find the list of all cryptocurrencies ranked based on their market cap at any given time here: coinmarketcap.com and coingecko.com.

1. Bitcoin (BTC)
2. Ethereum (ETH)
3. Tether (USDT)
4. Binance Coin (BNB)
5. Solana (SOL)
6. USDC (USDC)
7. Ripple (XRP)
8. Dogecoin (DOGE)
9. Toncoin (TON)
10. Cardano (ADA)
11. Shiba Inu (SHIB)
12. Avalanche (AVAX)
13. Polkadot (DOT)
14. ChainLink (LINK)
15. TRON (TRX)
16. Bitcoin Cash (BCH)
17. Near Protocol (NEAR)
18. Polygon (MATIC)
19. Pepe (PEPE)
20. Uniswao (UNI)
21. Litecoin (LTC)
22. Internet Computer (ICP)

23. UNUS SED LEO (LEO)

24. Dai (DAI)

25. Ethereum Classic (ETC)

26. Aptos (APT)

27. Render (RNDR)

28. Hedera (HBAR)

29. Immutable (IMX)

30. Mantle (MNT)

31. Cosmos (ATOM)

32. Kaspa (KAS)

33. Filecoin (FIL)

34. Arbitrum (ARB)

35. Dogwifhat (WIF)

36. Cronos (CRO)

37. Stellar (XLM)

38. First digital USD (FDUSD)

39. The Graph (GRT)

40. Bittensor (TAO)

41. Stacks (STX)

42. OKB (OKB)

43. Optimism (OP)

44. Monero (XMR)

45. Maker (MKR)

46. Vechain (VET)

47. Arweave (AR)

48. Floki (FLOKI)

49. Bonk (BONK)

50. Sui (SUI)

We have to bear in mind that the rank of a cryptocurrency is dependent on various factors changing under different circumstances and not just a market capitalization. You can't go by what you see on the websites, and sometimes scammers pump it and dump the cryptocurrency, so it fosters the need to do some fundamental and technical analysis before you set out to choose crypto.

Keep a watch:

Here are some cryptocurrencies to watch out for in the RWA sector:

1. Ondo Finance - $ONDO

2. Clear Pool Finance - $CPOOL

3. Realio Network - $RIO

Not financial advice, but these are just my personal favorites and are for learning purposes.

Chapter 14

Different Types of Sectors

Here are some of the most popular cryptocurrency categories and the leading cryptocurrencies in each category. This information is based on their popularity and total market capitalization as of 2024. Some popular cryptocurrency categories include:

1. Decentralised Finance (DeFi)

2. Artificial Intelligence (AI)

3. Meme

4. Layer 1 and Layer 2 Scaling Solutions

5. Real-World Asset (RWA)

6. Decentralised Physical Infrastructure Networks (DePIN)

7. Gaming (GameFi)

8. Non-Fungible Tokens (NFTs)

9. Metaverse and Web 3

10. Stablecoins

Let's discuss in detail the top 5 hot sectors that are expected to perform exceptionally well in the coming years:

Decentralised Finance (DeFi)

Decentralized Finance (DeFi) is an emerging financial system that operates independently of traditional centralized institutions like banks and governments. It uses blockchain platforms such as Ethereum and Solana, employing smart contracts and decentralized applications (dApps) to carry out different financial services. It's that global, open, and permissionless alternative built on traditions from traditional finance (TradFi), not using various intermediaries, hence accessible and transparent, among other things.

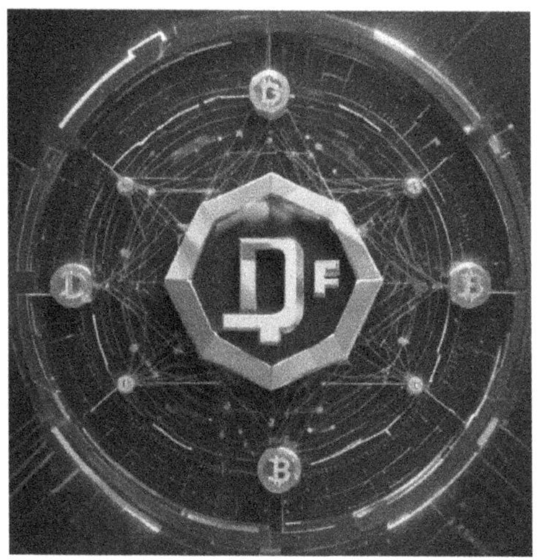

DeFi vs. TradFi

Traditional Finance (TradFi):

Traditional Finance operates under centralized control, meaning banks, stock exchanges, or insurance companies, within a regulated framework.

- **Intermediaries:** Transactions and risks are intermediated, adding costs and layers of bureaucracy.

- **Access:** Millions worldwide lack access to bank accounts and financial services.
- **Data Privacy:** Central systems access personal data and could block access to funds.

Decentralized Finance (DeFi):

- **Decentralized Operations:** Functions globally on a distributed system of computers, with no central control point.
- **No Middlemen:** Enables direct interaction without central intermediaries.
- **Free Access:** Open to anyone with internet access, without requiring identity verification.
- **Data Protection:** Users control their assets and personal data; transactions cannot be censored.

Critical Elements and Principles of DeFi

Financial Products

- **Lending and Borrowing:** DeFi protocols automate lending and borrowing using smart contracts, minimizing the role of middlemen.
- **Trading:** Decentralized exchanges allow direct peer-to-peer trades, reducing associated costs.
- **Yield Farming:** Users can earn rewards for providing liquidity in DeFi protocols.

Censorship Resistance:

- Transactions cannot be altered or suppressed by governments or third parties.
- DeFi systems operate under predefined rules, which, once established, cannot be retrospectively modified.

Innovation and Modularity:

- DeFi protocols can be combined to create new products and services ("money Legos").
- Community ownership and revenue sharing foster innovation and cooperation.

Example of Censorship Resistance in DeFi

In February 2022, the Canadian government froze protesters' bank accounts without a court order, demonstrating the need for decentralization. DeFi accounts are less susceptible to such centralized power, protecting the use and control of funds.

Risks and Challenges

While DeFi offers many advantages, several risks exist:

- **Smart Contract Security Risks:** Smart contracts can be buggy and exploitable.
- **User Responsibility:** Users must manage their resources independently, with no central body to indemnify or offer remedies in case of loss.
- **Regulatory Uncertainty:** The regulatory status of DeFi is still developing, impacting growth and adoption.

Here are some examples of DeFi Cryptos:

Token	Description	Use Case
Uniswap (UNI)	Governs the Uniswap decentralized exchange (DEX).	UNI holders can vote on proposals related to fees, liquidity pools, and new features for the Uniswap protocol.
Aave (AAVE)	Governs the Aave decentralized lending protocol.	AAVE holders can vote on proposals concerning interest rates, collateral requirements, and supported assets on the Aave platform.
Chainlink (LINK)	Powers the Chainlink decentralized oracle network.	LINK tokens are used to pay for secure and reliable data feeds that connect smart contracts to real-world information, enabling functionalities like automated payments and decentralized insurance.

Export to Sheets

DeFi represents a generational overhaul within the realm of finance, providing an all-inclusive, transparent and efficient system. The purpose of this is to recognize the differences or peculiarities the innovation offers over the traditional financial system that would afford greater financial freedom and innovation to humanity at large. Great, yet caution is necessary as generally with all DeFi-related investments, due to the natural risks and regulatory changes changing fast in DeFi.

Artificial Intelligence (AI)

Artificial intelligence combined with cryptocurrency is a domain of the future. It combines the capabilities of blockchain with AI potential to revolutionize a number of sectors. This is the way AI gets assimilated in the cryptocurrency space.

Increased fraud detection and security: AI algorithms scan vast amounts of market data in real-time, identify trading opportunities, and place the trades. These algorithms can identify patterns and, even making predictions that are not within human ability.

Sentiment Analysis: AI tools read through news, social media, among others, to gauge market sentiment and predict the movement of prices.

Fraud Detection and Security:

Anomaly Detection: By monitoring user behavior as well as blockchain transactions, AI systems are capable of detecting irregular patterns considered to be potential fraudulent activities, like money laundering or attempts to hack a system.

Improves Security: Machine learning algorithms could improve the security of the blockchain network by predicting the attack and recognizing the system's vulnerabilities.

Smart Contracts and dApps:

Automated Contract Execution: Even more automation of sophisticated associated smart contract functions, meaning that they become more adaptive and responsive to complex conditions.

Improved dApp Performance: Make decentralized applications efficient and enhance the performance via the optimization of usage patterns and dynamic resource allocation for better efficiency in decentralized applications.

NLP and Customer Support

AI Chatbots: AI chatbots make sure there is instant customer support to look after all questions and solutions of the user on the cryptocurrency platform.

Automated Reporting: To automatically create reports and insights from the data, it would save so much of the time of the user and help them understand the investment performance and market trends in the easiest ways possible.

Benefits and Challenges

Benefits

- Efficiency: The speed at which AI can process and analyze large datasets allows it to quickly pull out insights that help in making faster and more efficient decisions and the processing of operations.
- Security: Protects blockchain networks by increased detection of fraud and anomaly detection.
- Accessibility: Therefore, AI-powered tools are to present complex financial services in an accessible

form for a wide audience—even clients without financial literacy at advanced levels.

Drawbacks

- Complexity: The integration of AI with blockchain technology would be technically difficult and hired expertise.
- Privacy: The problem of privacy and security user data in AI-driven applications.
- Regulation: The regulatory environment for both AI and blockchain, being new and ever-adapting, can have an effect on the creation and use of AI-based cryptocurrency solutions.

Here are some examples of AI Cryptos:

Token	Description	Use Case
Ocean Protocol (OCEAN)	Facilitates data sharing and monetization for AI development.	OCEAN creates a marketplace where users can buy and sell access to valuable datasets needed to train AI models.
SingularityNET (AGI)	Supports the development of a decentralized AI marketplace.	AGI focuses on building a platform where developers can collaborate and create, share, and monetize AI services and applications.
Fetch.ai (FET)	Powers a decentralized machine learning network.	FET tokens incentivize users to contribute data and computing power for training AI models on the Fetch.ai network.

Export to Sheets

Merging the potential of AI with cryptocurrencies is a new wedge of innovation. One that will allow us to embrace new ways of enhancing all these three pillars related to financial services, security, and user experience. With the mature technology of AI, we are going to see more sophisticated AI application in the cryptocurrencies business, which will drive the decentralized finance space and be on the radar.

MEME

A meme coin is a subset of digital assets inspired by internet memes, cultural trends, or humorous content. Often created as jokes, these coins can unexpectedly gain substantial value due to their community support and viral potential. Let's take a holistic view of the meme coin sector in cryptocurrency:

Key Characteristics of Meme Cryptocurrencies

Community-Driven:

- Robust Communities: Meme coins are backed by active and lively communities, increasing demand and popularity. Social media platforms like Reddit, Twitter, and Discord are key for discussion and promotion.
- Viral Marketing: The success of meme coins often relies on their viral nature, with memes, jokes, and funny content rapidly boosting visibility and attractiveness.

Speculative Nature:

- Volatility: Meme cryptos are highly volatile, with price fluctuations driven by speculation and market hype rather than intrinsic value or technological innovation.
- Pump-and-Dump Schemes: Due to their speculative nature, meme coins are prone to pump-and-dump schemes, where prices are artificially inflated and then rapidly sold off.

Lack of Utility:

- Limited Practical Use: Most meme coins have little or no practical use compared to other cryptocurrencies; their value is primarily derived from community interest and speculative trading.
- Fun and Entertainment: Despite limited utility, meme coins provide entertainment and social capital for their holders.

Accessibility and Ease of Trading:

- Low-Effort Creation: Meme coins are often created with minimal technical investment. They can be launched on popular blockchain platforms like Ethereum and Binance Smart Chain using standard token protocols.
- Reduced Prices and Easy Access: Lower prices and easy access attract new and casual investors to the cryptocurrency world.
- Community Engagement: Meme coins foster a sense of belonging and amusement among their owners.
- Easy Accessibility: The reduced capital barriers make it easy for first-time investors to enter the cryptocurrency ecosystem.

- Potential Profit: Early adopters can potentially make significant profits if a meme coin gains real value.

Threats:

- High Risk: Due to their speculative nature, meme coins are highly volatile, with prices swinging dramatically based on market sentiment and hype.
- Lack of Fundamental Value: Most meme coins lack solid technology or utility, making them susceptible to market manipulation and transient popularity.
- Regulatory Scrutiny: Meme coins could attract regulatory attention, especially if involved in pump-and-dump schemes or other fraudulent activities.

Here are some examples of MEME Cryptos:

Token	Description	Use Case
Dogecoin (DOGE)	Started as a joke referencing a popular meme featuring a Shiba Inu dog.	Originally intended as a satirical take on cryptocurrencies, Dogecoin has developed a large and passionate community. It's sometimes used for tipping content creators and for online microtransactions.
Shiba Inu (SHIB)	Inspired by the Dogecoin meme and features a similar Shiba Inu dog logo.	SHIB capitalizes on the popularity of Dogecoin and leverages a similar meme-based community. It's used for online payments and potentially within the ShibaSwap decentralized exchange (DEX).
Floki Inu (FLOKI)	Another meme token inspired by the Dogecoin craze, featuring a cartoon image of Elon Musk's dog, Floki.	FLOKI relies heavily on community engagement and social media hype. It's used for online payments and might be integrated into future play-to-earn games.

Export to Sheets

Meme cryptocurrencies represent a unique and exciting segment of the market. Although they often start as jokes or parodies, their potential for virality and strong community support can lead to significant market activity. Despite their high volatility and speculative nature, meme coins continue to capture the imagination and engagement of crypto enthusiasts worldwide, highlighting the dynamic and diverse nature of the cryptocurrency ecosystem.

Real World Assets (RWA)

The RWA sector in cryptocurrency involves the tokenization and integration of tangible assets or traditional financial instruments into blockchain ecosystems. Issuing RWAs with blockchain technology interconnects the physical and digital worlds, making assets more tradable while ensuring transparency and access.

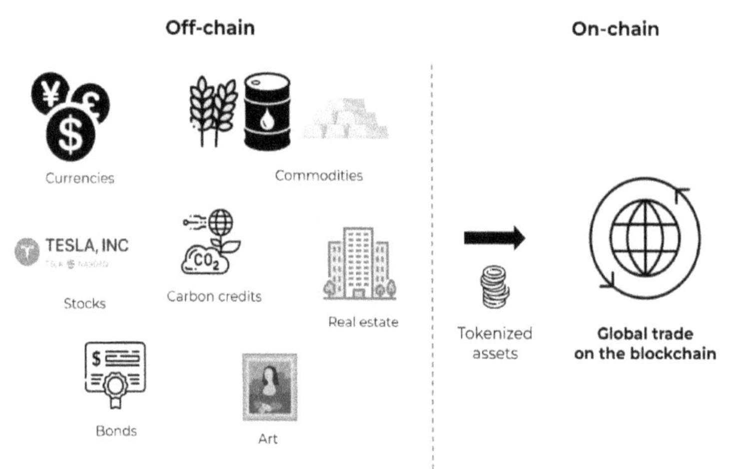

Features of RWA:

- Assets: Examples include real estate, commodities, bonds, stocks, art, and others.
- Liquidity:

- o Improved Liquidity: Asset tokenization enhances liquidity by enabling the buying and selling of tokens in the secondary market, improving the liquidity of traditionally illiquid assets.

- Fractional Ownership: Investors can own fractions of high-value assets, making investment more accessible and diversified.

- Transparency and Security:

  - o Blockchain Ledger: All transactions and ownership rights are securely recorded on a blockchain and are publicly accessible, reducing the possibility of fraud.
  - o Immutable Records: Blockchain's decentralized nature ensures that asset records are tamper-proof and auditable.

- Accessibility:

  - o Global Market: Tokenized assets can be traded globally 24/7, opening up markets to both investors and assets.
  - o Lower Barriers: Lower entry costs and minimal intermediaries allow more people to invest in assets that were previously less accessible.

- Smart Contracts:

  - o Automated Processes: Smart contracts automate processes such as dividend payments, interest accrual, and ownership transfer, saving administrative costs and eliminating inefficiencies.

Examples of Real-World Asset Projects:

Real Estate:

Platforms: Companies like RealT and Propy enable real estate tokenization for buying and selling fractional shares of properties.

Benefits: Investors can diversify their portfolios with stakes in multiple properties and benefit from potential rental income or price appreciation.

Commodities:

Tokenized Gold: Projects like Paxos and Digix tokenize gold, allowing people to own and trade gold as a digital asset without needing physical storage.

Advantages: Token holders can easily trade gold-backed tokens on various exchanges, creating a liquid market for precious metals.

Art and Collectibles:

Platforms: Platforms like Maecenas and NFT marketplaces enables the tokenization of fine art and collectibles, allowing investors to own shares in valuable pieces.

Art Market: Investors can access the art market without needing significant capital to purchase entire pieces.

Bonds and Stocks:

Synthetic Assets: Projects like Synthetix and Mirror Protocol offer synthetic assets that mimic the value of financial instruments, allowing decentralized trading of these assets.

Flexibility: Digital assets are tradable around the clock, providing liquidity and efficiency through blockchain technology.

Challenges and Considerations:

- Regulatory Compliance:

  - Regulatory Frameworks: Divergent regulatory environments in various jurisdictions pose a major challenge.
  - Compliance: Tokenized assets must conform to existing laws for securities, AML, and KYC.

- Valuation and Price Discovery:

  - Proper Valuation: Correctly valuing tokenized assets, especially unique or illiquid ones, is challenging.
  - Market Dynamics: Fair and transparent price discovery mechanisms are essential to maintain market integrity.

- Security and Custody:

  - Asset Custody: Secure custody of both real-world assets and their digital representations is crucial.
  - Smart Contract Risks: Ensuring the security of smart contracts and blockchain infrastructure is paramount to avoid hacks and unauthorized access.

- Market Adoption:

  - Education: Customers must be educated on the benefits and risks associated with tokenized assets.
  - Infrastructure: Developing secure wallets and compliant exchanges is necessary to support the ecosystem.

Here are some examples of RWA Cryptos:

RWA Type	Cryptocurrency Example	Description
Real Estate	St Real Estate (REX)	REX tokens represent ownership in a portfolio of real-world properties managed by the St Real Estate platform. Investors can gain exposure to the real estate market without directly purchasing physical property.
Stocks	SharesToken (SHARE)	SHARE tokens represent fractional ownership of shares in publicly traded companies. This allows investors to buy a fraction of a share, potentially lowering the barrier to entry for certain stocks.
Commodities	Tether Gold (XAUT)	Each XAUT token is backed by one physical ounce of gold stored in a secure vault. Investors can gain exposure to the gold market through a cryptocurrency token.

The RWA sector in cryptocurrency has been a breakthrough in the digital economy, integrating tangible assets through tokenization. This integration brings high liquidity, transparency, and ease of access, allowing more investors to participate in these markets. However, challenges around regulatory compliance, valuation, and security must still be addressed. The potential benefits place RWAs in a promising position for continued growth and development within the cryptocurrency space.

Decentralized Physical Infrastructure Networks (DePIN)

DePIN is an emerging sector in the cryptocurrency and blockchain industry. Utilizing blockchains and smart contracts, DePIN projects aim to decentralize the ownership, operation, and management of physical infrastructure.

This approach applies to various types of physical assets, including telecommunications, energy, transportation, and environmental monitoring infrastructures.

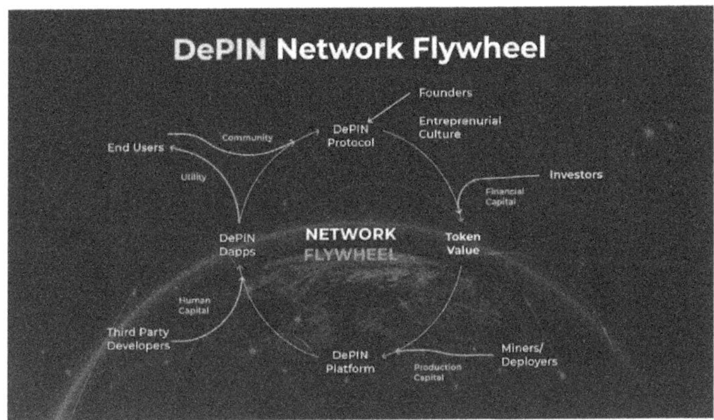

Source: Coingecko

Main Features and Advantages of DePIN:

Decentralization:

Community Ownership: DePIN projects enable community ownership and management of physical infrastructure, reducing reliance on centralized entities.

Distributed Control: Decentralized networks distribute control among multiple stakeholders, increasing resilience and reducing single points of failure.

Tokenization:

Incentives: Tokens are provided to incentivize participants to contribute resources such as bandwidth, storage, or energy to the network.

Governance: Token holders can influence network direction and policy, providing a mechanism for decentralized governance.

Transparency and Security:

Immutable Data: Blockchain technology ensures that data related to infrastructure operations is immutable, transparent, tamper-proof, and easily auditable.

Smart Contracts: Automated processes via smart contracts eliminate intermediaries, enhancing security and efficiency.

Efficiency and Cost Reduction:

Resource Optimization: Decentralized networks dynamically allocate resources based on demand, increasing efficiency.

Reduced Operational Costs: Eliminating intermediaries and utilizing community resources significantly reduce operational costs.

Challenges and Considerations:

Regulatory Compliance:

- Regulations: Utilities and telecommunications infrastructures are subject to various regulations.
- Compliance Costs: Ensuring decentralized networks comply with legislation and local regulations can be costly.

Scalability:

- Network Growth: Maintaining network effectiveness and security requires significant effort as DePIN networks grow.
- Resource Allocation: Advanced algorithms and protocols are needed for optimal resource allocation within the growing network.

- Integration: Decentralized networks must integrate with existing centralized infrastructure and services.
- Standards: Common standards for interoperability are essential for successful DePIN projects.

User Adoption:

- Awareness and Education: Potential users must be informed and educated about the benefits and workings of DePIN networks to promote widespread adoption.
- Usability: User-friendly interfaces and straightforward designs are crucial for user acceptance of decentralized networks.

Here are some examples of DePIN Cryptos:

Real-World Asset	Cryptocurrency Example	Description
Wireless Network Infrastructure	Helium (HNT)	HNT tokens incentivize users to share their wireless network coverage by installing Helium hotspots. These hotspots provide internet connectivity for low-powered devices in the internet of Things (IoT) ecosystem.
Cloud Computing Resources	Render Token (RNDR)	RNDR tokens allow users to buy and sell access to computing power for rendering 3D graphics, video editing, and other computationally intensive tasks. This creates a decentralized marketplace for cloud computing resources.
Electric Vehicle Charging Stations	MOVE Network (MOVE)	(Hypothetical Example) MOVE tokens could be used to pay for electric vehicle charging at stations participating in a DePIN network. Token holders could also potentially earn rewards for providing charging infrastructure or contributing to network governance.

DePIN represents a new paradigm in managing and operating physical infrastructure through decentralization and blockchain technologies. DePIN projects have the potential to revolutionize sectors such as telecommunications, energy, and storage by promoting community ownership, increasing transparency, and reducing costs. Despite challenges related to regulatory compliance, scalability, and user adoption, the prospective development in the DePIN sector remains promising, poised to bring forward efficient, resilient, and inclusive infrastructure networks.

Part 5
DYOR

Chapter 15
DYOR Analysis

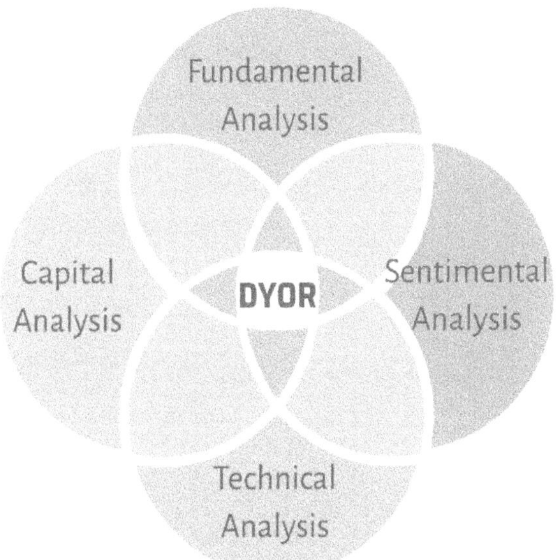

For instance, many individual investors typically learn one or two methods for analyzing the markets before making investment decisions. For example, new investors often use technical analysis and rely on their favorite economic news anchors on TV. However, relying on one type of analysis can be very risky, which is where the "Do Your Own Research" (DYOR) Analysis comes in.

The DYOR recommends analyzing the markets from four different points.

1. Capital Analysis

2. Sentiment Analysis

3. Fundamental Analysis

4. Technical Analysis

Fundamental Analysis

Definition: Fundamental analysis involves assessing the intrinsic value of a cryptocurrency based on various fundamental factors.

Key Aspects:

Project Fundamentals: Evaluating the whitepaper, use case, team expertise, partnerships, and roadmap to gauge the project's potential.

Technology: Understanding the underlying blockchain platform, consensus mechanism, scalability solutions, and technological innovations.

Utility and Adoption: Assessing real-world applications and adoption rates within the industry to determine the cryptocurrency's practical value.

On-chain Data: Analyzing blockchain metrics such as transaction volume, active addresses, and network activity to understand user engagement.

Regulation and Compliance: Considering regulatory implications and compliance requirements that could impact the project's future viability.

Market Position and Competition: Comparing the cryptocurrency's market position relative to competitors and assessing competitive dynamics.

Objective: Fundamental analysis helps investors identify cryptocurrencies with strong long-term potential based on their underlying value and market positioning.

Technical Analysis

Definition: Technical analysis involves studying historical price data to forecast future price movements and identify trading opportunities.

Tools and Techniques:

Price Charts: Examining historical price patterns, trends, and key levels of support and resistance to identify potential entry and exit points.

Indicators and Oscillators: Using technical indicators like moving averages, RSI, MACD, and Bollinger Bands to analyze price momentum and predict trend reversals.

Volume Analysis: Analyzing trading volumes to confirm price trends and gauge the strength of market movements.

Candlestick Patterns: Recognizing candlestick patterns such as Doji, Hammer, and Engulfing patterns to predict potential price reversals or continuations.

Objective: Technical analysis assists in timing trades and optimizing entry and exit points based on market behavior and price action signals.

Sentimental Analysis

Definition: Sentimental analysis focuses on understanding markets sentiment and investor emotions surrounding a cryptocurrency.

Key Components:

Market Sentiment: Assessing whether the market sentiment towards a cryptocurrency is bullish (positive) or bearish (negative).

News and Social Media: Monitoring news outlets, social media platforms, and forums for shifts in public opinion and sentiment-related news.

Fear and Greed Index: Using sentiment indices like the Crypto Fear and Greed Index to gauge overall market sentiment and sentiment extremes.

Community Engagement: Evaluating developer activity, user engagement, and community sentiment to gauge support for a cryptocurrency.

Objective: Sentimental analysis helps predict how market participants are likely to react to news, events, or market developments, influencing future price movements.

Integration and Decision-making

By combining fundamental, technical, and sentimental analyses, investors gain a comprehensive understanding of a cryptocurrency's potential. This integrated approach allows for:

- **Identifying Strong Projects:** Fundamental analysis identifies cryptocurrencies with robust fundamentals and long-term viability.
- **Optimizing Entry and Exit Points:** Technical analysis assists in timing trades to maximize profitability and manage risk.
- **Forecasting Market Reactions:** Sentimental analysis provides insights into market sentiment and potential reactions to news or events.

Investing Basics 101

Volatality

This is the price movement rate—price going both upwards and downwards—in the asset. Given that the speed and degree of the price movements this indicator captures, volatility is often used to measure the risk of investing an asset. Most Cryptocurrencies are considerably more volatile than most classes of assets, for various reasons. These are due to current low levels of regulation, and the market size is still relatively small.

A lot of times, people use volatility to describe risk when it is not the same thing. They are two different things. Risk is chances of loss. Volatility describes how much and how fast a price moves. If the price movements also raised your chances of loss, then that amounts to raising the risk just the same.

But here's the thing—volatility really isn't essentially a good or bad attribute. It really can mean the potential for massive upsides. That is, if an asset really rises in value, it's volatile to the upside; if it really decreases in value, it's volatile to the downside.

It's all that matters: whether it's going in the right direction for you or not. For example, you would want to go short on an asset really if it were to go down in value. As long as it's going in the right direction, you'd want an asset to be volatile.

The greater interest in investing in cryptocurrency partially results from its greater level of volatility, which means that an investor will be able to realize much returns over relatively short periods.

But naturally, high volatility entails lots of risks, and below we will get closer to how to work with the risks and minimize losses. Anyway, volatility in the crypto markets should decrease with growth, mass adoption, and regulation.

What is diversification?

Diversification stands for the spread of capital through various types of coins and tokens. There is a need to create a portfolio spanning a wide range of assets from a wide range of sectors.

Part of learning not to lose too much is in respect to learning how to balance the risk because such a market can be highly volatile to invest. But then, the portfolio has to be diversified into different assets and sectors so that the threat on failure in each is distributed. But if one asset doesn't perform to expectations of being a good investment, another loss will be limited to the capital allocation of that particular asset.

An investor would go for some high-returning, at the same time high-risk assets that pay well off in bull markets, but also for some lower-risk, lower-reward papers that also wouldn't suffocate from bear markets.

Key would be diversifying out of one type of asset, for example, cross-chain assets or derivatives, so that when regulation or working with a better solution gets in the way, you don't lose everything.

In the event a person is worried about heavy investments in single or a similar asset or is under-diversified, they may incur a loss or lose everything even in conditions where the market is doing well. In a diversified portfolio, the positive-performing assets tend to offset those with poor or negative returns.

Example: if an overall portfolio was invested with 10% in 10 different assets and one asset goes to 0, then the loss will be 10%. But if, say, 300% goes up of a asset to the top, which is not very uncommon for any crypto asset to give during a run to the top, then the overall portfolio will gain 30% with a maximum worst-case of a 10% risk in the case all other do not lose much if at all when part of the money has been transferred to the rocketing asset.

The trick of investment is that you can never have a sure way out of losing every single dime.

In the real world, yes, some will go up, some will go down, but an investor with balance in their investments at the end of the day should end up finding good returns with limited downside risk.

The general reason why diversification is key: in financial markets, nobody knows anything for sure, notwithstanding how confident the investor may be within any investment.

Note that over-diversification is also very possible. If an investor is investing in too many assets, the returns will be insignificant as the capital gets spread too thinly.

It is all about intelligent diversification. For instance, being invested in oil and gas, one would invest in some high-potential renewable energy stocks, apart from assets outside the energy sector, such as Bitcoin and Gold.

Dollar-cost average (DCA)

Dollar-cost average, or DCA, is an investment strategy of buying an asset at a fixed time interval continuously, rather than in one go or at one stroke.

At the onset, an investor would decide to invest a certain amount totally, and then he would make his investment in small, equal parts either at a predetermined time or at an anticipated price.

For example, an investor who has $500 to invest can pour in $100 each month and not all $500 at one time.

Just as it is hard to time the market, one should not expect to do so. DCA takes time out of the equation. No one catches the absolute top or bottom, but when putting in larger investments, price fluctuations do matter.

This will serve to decrease the impact of volatility and thus decrease the risk of making an ill-timed investment. It also decreases the impact of emotions on your decision.

Assuming you are not a full-time investor or trader, you for sure cannot know everything happening around the world. There are always huge unknowns which will have a huge impact on prices and dollar-cost averaging into an asset reduces the risks arising from that.

However, it doesn't remove the risk since the idea is just to minimize the risk of bad timing. Other factors also have to be considered.

What is unique about DCA, relevant in this context with time? Realizing that DCA is usually done at a time of panic and stress in the market, when things are undervalued, many people might do it sporadically. However, in crypto, one may opt to always DCA insofar as they are in it for the long haul because, in this inventory, prospects of growth are indeed very high.

DCA can definitely help a person buy low and sell high by purchasing when others are selling. However, DCA is not only useful "on the way in." One can employ DCA "on the way out" as well, upon taking a profit. It's practically impossible to catch the absolute bottom, but DCA offers a way to remove timing at the end.

Let us calculate Profit from DCAing into BTC over the last 10 years with the help of ChatGPT. **(Results are based on ChatGPT so that you can try it out by yourself by asking with ChatGPT)**

Dollar-Cost Averaging (DCA) into Bitcoin (BTC) over the last 10 years would have yielded varying profits depending on the timing and frequency of investments. To calculate an approximate profit, let's consider a simple example:

Assume you start investing $100 every month into Bitcoin over the past 10 years. We'll use the following historical prices as a rough estimate:

June 2014: ~$600

June 2015: ~$250

June 2016: ~$700

June 2017: ~$2,500

June 2018: ~$6,000

June 2019: ~$8,000

June 2020: ~$9,000

June 2021: ~$35,000

June 2022: ~$40,000 (approximate)

These are just rough estimates, and the actual prices varied throughout each year. However, for simplicity, let's assume you invest $100 at the closing price of Bitcoin on the 15th of each month over the last 10 years.

Here's a simplified calculation:

1. Calculate the number of months over 10 years: 10 years * 12 months/year = 120 months.

2. Total investment made: $100 * 120 months = $12,000.

Now, assuming you bought Bitcoin at the closing price each month, you'd own a certain amount of Bitcoin. To find the profit, you'd compare the current value of your Bitcoin holdings with the initial investment of $12,000.

Let's assume Bitcoin's price in June 2024 is $40,000 (hypothetical for calculation purposes):

- Value of Bitcoin holdings = (Amount of Bitcoin owned) * $40,000.

If the value of Bitcoin holdings after 10 years is $50,000, for instance, then:

- Profit = Value of Bitcoin holdings - Total investment
- Profit = $50,000 - $12,000
- Profit = $38,000.

So, in this hypothetical scenario, DCAing $100 per month into Bitcoin over the last 10 years could result in a profit of $38,000, assuming the current Bitcoin price is $40,000. Actual profits would vary based on the actual timing and prices at which investments were made.

What is opportunity cost?

Opportunity cost is the potential benefit that an individual misses out on when they choose one option over another. These costs are often unseen and thus easy to overlook. Understanding the potential missed opportunities when choosing one investment over another enables better, more profitable decision-making.

For instance, if you choose to buy a $5 coffee today, you forego the opportunity to spend that $5 in other ways today and in the future, and you also miss out on the benefit of saving $5 regularly.

To properly evaluate opportunity costs, you must consider and compare the costs and benefits of all available options. When making an investment decision, consider the potential benefits of each option and what you will have to give up in the present and future by choosing that option (the cost of the path not taken).

For example, you may need to choose between selling your assets now for immediate gains or holding onto them for potential future gains. Opportunity cost is not an exact calculation, but you can estimate the difference between the potential returns of each available option using the formula:

OPPORTUNITY COST = RETURN FROM THE MOST PROFITABLE OPTION – RETURN FROM CHOSEN OPTION.

Considering and comparing the costs and benefits of every available option is essential for evaluating opportunity costs properly, as every decision involves losses and gains. It requires thinking long-term, as short-term gains may not always lead to long-term growth.

What is passive income?

Passive Income is most certainly the very cornerstone of investing and making money in general—it is why the rich are rich! At its most basic, earning a passive income involves investing money into something that will generate some sort of an income, or a "yield".

The term "yield" is given to the financial return that a particular investment strategy gives. Its profits are what you make from that strategy. It comes from many different things, all of which have different rewards and risk profiles.

Cryptos yield many ways to create passive income, such as through yield farming, staking, and lending.

Lending

The most basic source of yield is lending.

Lending implies a depositor who lends out his or her assets to earn a yield, something that will later become payable by the same borrowers. Borrowing this asset is done by the borrower, as it offers them leverage on their exposure and thus potential higher returns. Generally, leverage is a form of investment strategy that uses borrowed money to increase the potential return of an investment.

It is important to first spend time understanding the given platform's risk profile.

Yield farming

Yield farming is the process of generating rewards with crypto asset holdings. In simple terms, it means putting your $CRYPTO into work and earning rewards. Most commonly, it involves users, called liquidity providers (LPs), supplying liquidity to liquidity pools.

Liquidity refers to converting an asset into another asset without causing any changes to the market value of the first asset. Liquidity pools are simply pooling two or more digital assets. Liquidity pools allow anyone to provide liquidity by depositing the assets or take liquidity be puling/selling the assets.

By depositing money within a crypto exchange, liquidity is made available. And, in turn, the depositor is paid a part of the transaction. In some instances, the depositors can even get more rewards added to their returns from the transaction. In the form of the exchange's native token.

Through this further reward, one is said to be "yield farming." This has the potential to make more money liquid for shorter periods.

Now while this sounds very lucrative, it needs to be understood that there are potential risks in providing liquidity. This includes the concept called "impermanent loss" that we can detail as a form of opportunity cost that it pays while providing liquidity.

One of the risks that come along with using liquidity pools is impermanent loss. This will occur when liquidity is provided to the pool but the deposited assets' prices will change from what they were when deposited.

Being that liquidity provision results in this impermanent loss, the liquidity value will be lower than if one just held the tokens.

Staking

Basically, on PoS blockchains, such as Ethereum or Solana, anybody can take part in the security process by "staking" their ETH or SOL. For further details, you can become well-informed about proof of stake in Module 2.

Essentially, staking activity consists of running validator hardware, needed to do the work of verifying transactions. For those who do not have the resources to run a validator individually, there are staking pools.

A staking pool is just the amalgamation of individual crypto deposits into a collective pool run by a subset of validators. Over time, those staking rewards are paid out in the native token of the blockchain—I suppose SOL for Solana or ETH on Ethereum.

Note that, although you can stake, it will not secure the network. PoS is when you secure the network because that is the consensus mechanism. Many protocols will do this through staking in the way of locking up token supply to push the price up artificially, with no value added back into the ecosystem. This is kind of a red flag but is generally found throughout the whole of crypto.

Annual percentage yield (APY)

$$APY = (1 + r/n)\, n - 1$$

Annual Percentage Yield or APY is the actual rate of return on investment, taking into account compound interest. Compound interest is periodically added, increasing the total. This means that each interest rate with be higher, based on the higher total amount.

r = period rate

n = number of compounding periods

For example, an investor is comparing an investment that pays 6% annually and an investment that pays 0.5% per month with monthly compounding.

At first glance, the yields appear the same because 12 months multiplied by 0.5% is 6%.

However, when the effects of compounding are taken into account by calculating the APY, the money market investment actually yields $(1 + .005) \wedge 12 - 1 = 0.06168 = 6.17\%$.

Annual Percentage Rate (APR)

An annual percentage rate (APR) is the annual rate earned by an investment. APR only accounts for simple interest, the annual percentage yield (APY) takes compound interest into account.

What is compound interest?

Compounded interest is often said to be "interest on interest." It is, in fact, the interest received on an original principal and already on other interest that has been added to the original amount.

Stakers usually harvest rewards and compound them back into the pool to earn more on the amount of the principal and, as a result, more on the rewards the next time. This process actually creates compound interest. Most auto-compounding is available in the majority of farms, considering that the yields are higher.

Compound interests bring about more benefit than simple interest (where there is not the combination of the accumulated interest with the initial amount).

Let's look at a basic example:

Remember the following information about compound interest:

In a savings account with a 5% annual interest rate, your $1000 would earn $50 in the first year, resulting in a new balance of $1050. In the second year, you would earn $52.50 bringing your balance to $1102.50. Over time, compound interest causes your balance to grow exponentially as you earn interest on an increasing amount.

If you leave the original $1000 in the savings account for 10 years, you'll end up with $1,629, after 20 years, $2,653, and after 50 years, $11,468. So it's clear that the earlier you start saving, the more your money can grow.

Remember, never invest more than you can afford to lose. It's important not to invest what you can't afford to lose, even if you believe strongly in crypto. Anything can happen.

Chapter 16

Fundamental Analysis

Fundamental analysis, in my opinion, means looking at all the information, rumors, and facts about this asset: the problem it solves, its long-term value proposition, relevance over your investment horizon, and particularly its financial health and upcoming risk events. Well, this could be applied to cryptocurrencies, too. Picking a category of crypto is a little bit like picking a significant other. When investing in cryptos, use your brain and maybe intuition, but nothing more. Here are some ways to help you pick the best crypto assets for investment.

Invest in what you know

Invest in what you know. Similar in the stock market. Now, if you've seen some of the cryptocurrencies and have experience using them, or in case you were using them and they seemed to be functioning well, then you can invest that. Similarly, in the stock market, many new investors have been able to make profitable investments by just observing their buying habits. They simply might want to add CMG to their portfolio because they only purchase from healthier fast-food services like Chipotle, on the New York Stock Exchange under the ticker CMG rather than patronizing a McDonald's, on the Big Board under MCD.

Also, if you find out that your online favorite store has put a cryptocurrency as a method of payment on the checkout page and you can order goods without problem using that cryptocurrency, it may be a signal that the trading volume of that cryptocurrency in the future will increase. Then cryptocurrency could be a very good asset for your portfolio.

Source: Tradesanta

Investing in what you know is my favorite strategy. Now, this is more than investing in online financial markets. Think of who you know the most about; who would that be? The person you know the most about in this entire world, most likely, is yourself. This is why, at the top level of the Invest Diva Movement, the first and foremost is investing in yourself. That can be your health or your relationships or learning high-income generation skills to enhance your wealth. When you're reading this book to learn about next-generation investing-congratulations-you invest in yourself. While you gather high-income-producing skills, no matter what turn the world or the economy takes, you will always be there for yourself.r yourself.

Fundamental analysis holds very important significance in the case of long-term investments. Ample time must be invested in research and analysis to understand the potential value growth of any particular project over the next months or years.

Let's explore the key aspects to consider during the fundamental analysis of a crypto project.

General Research

This will involve doing online research about the project using Google searches; this will involve putting the name of the asset and then going at least 5 pages deep in the Google search results. Open any interesting findings and ensure to use of different combinations of keywords. Also, look out for any individually written research articles by those not working for the project team to get a fuller understanding of the project.

Ask yourself:

1. Where does this project derive its value?
2. Does it have the potential for growth over time?
3. On which exchanges is the cryptocurrency available?
4. Who are the crypto's partners, and what do these partnerships signify?

Wallet Holders

Use a blockchain explorer like

https://etherscan.io/,
https://bscscan.com/,
https://solscan.io/,
https://arbiscan.io/

To check the distribution among the number of token holders; verify that no wallet/person has an unusually high amount - thus no whales are controlling it.

It's very risky if a high percentage of tokens belongs to a small group of investors or team members. There could be undue influence over governance, or the token price can be manipulated through pumping and dumping.

Project website

Please take note of the following instructions:

1. Go to the project's website and read all the links on that page. While an amazing website doesn't need to exist, a poorly designed site is usually a warning sign. Look for details- spelling and grammar errors are also usually not good signs.

2. The website should immediately explain what the project is, what its aim is, and what the value proposition is. If you struggle to understand the purpose of the project, or the information seems confusing or unclear, this is generally a bad sign.

3. Dive deep into the website of the project to know what is submitted, what the idea is, what is offered or promised, and whether they are keeping true to their words. More importantly, look for the reason why it should not be a good investment rather than trying to convince yourself it would certainly be, intensely. Look at it as a business: would you want that business?

4. Note the partnerships and backers for the project and their research on them. The alliances are crucial to add

value to a project. Still, considering any partnership, see the details of the tie-up before drawing judgment.

Ask yourself:

1. What is the website like?

2. Does the website clearly state the project's purpose?

3. Are there any red flags?

4. Who is the project partnered with?

Whitepaper

A whitepaper is used to expound on and market the information related to a given technical project. It is something that every cryptocurrency project must have when seeking legitimacy and starting in the market. Ever since Satoshi Nakamoto came out with the Bitcoin whitepaper in October 2008, these documents presented the rationale behind introducing a specific cryptocurrency, the problem it is intended to solve, and in what aspects it will be better/different than its nearest competitors. Understanding a whitepaper can be tricky. Jargon and buzzwords are normally used throughout which at times are hard to understand. Whitepapers were around long before cryptocurrency; they're just one avenue of explaining practically any kind of project. Still, they have become an industry standard for this fast-paced world. So, how do you read one, learn if it is a real-world fix situation one that is just a lot of fluff?

Common parts of a whitepaper

The next part includes features generally available while breaking down a whitepaper. Not every whitepaper will contain all features, and the information may be presented differently.

Abstract

An abstract is a digest which sits at the beginning of a whitepaper. Typically, objectives are introduced, and the reader is enticed to continue using the document.

Introduction

The chapter is expected to give a general brief mentioning of underlying concepts such as the definition of a real blockchain, while at the same time making it the first time the proposed solution for the actual cryptocurrency project is being introduced.

Contextual Definition of Problem

This should be the section where the development team starts building a case for the introduction of their novel solution—

some kind of cryptocurrency. The key contents should be details about the targeted market of the project, the problems to be solved, and the criticisms of the existing solutions.

Solution/Product Description

First came explaining the problem and discussing the deficits in the solutions existing at the moment. A bit later, it went on to describe the way the development team saw a solution to the problem, its specific features, the platform on which this kind of solution will be implemented, and how it will beat everything that exists now.

Next, in the following section, the technical specifications of the project, tools, and programming languages used in creating the solution are expounded.

Both the token and the tokenomics are the most important things for potential investors and therefore explicitly explained in great detail. This section of the whitepaper provides the utility that the token will have in the project's ecosystem processes, its governance structure, the benefits of holding it, and the proposed use cases of the token.

Lastly, the whitepaper familiarizes readers with the team of the project, where readers can know the past experiences of the team, how many years of experience they each have in the field and the position that each one holds in the whole team.

A whitepaper is, in fact, a sort of marketing document. Toward the end, it sometimes contains a section on "how to buy your token" that includes launch dates, exchanges, and wallet addresses—for maximum transparency, of course.

Project roadmap

The team must have spelled out a future project vision. This may be how many holders the project should have or listing on centralized exchanges with a general time frame to complete said milestones.

Conclusion

This is pretty clear, indeed. This section contains a summary of the project, also a call to action, and a problem the project proposed to be resolved.

While reading a whitepaper

Contrary to what most individuals might consider when going through a whitepaper, there's a general set of questions to validate the legitimacy of a project, regardless of the nature of that project. Four of them, in this regard, are as follows:

1. What is the goal of this project?
2. How does the project plan to achieve its goal?
3. Is there a genuine need for this project to utilize blockchain technology?
4. Does the project have a skilled team with a proven track record of delivering results?

While these questions don't cover everything, they provide a solid foundation for individuals new to cryptocurrency, whitepapers, or investing in general.

Next steps after reading the whitepaper

It is worth remembering that a whitepaper represents the opinion of the team behind the project regarding its goals and the benefits that it is supposed to bring. However, more often than not, whitepapers act as marketing tools for such projects and their teams, selling the reader the idea that their project is the best. Because at times, they are biased from a certain angle, one must conduct elaborate research before making heavy investments in any coin or token. One way to verify claims made in a whitepaper is to read and check articles by people not affiliated with a particular project and pursue outside sources.

In the end, the idea is to simply have done enough research to be confident about a project and to be able to justify why it is a good investment. Knowing how to analyze a whitepaper is a good place to start researching a project. It can help one feel safe in the investment decision, even with the presence of fear, uncertainty, and doubt, and the downward movements in price.

Team

Research the team and the history. Actually, it is the team that drives the crypto project. Therefore, they are vital to its success. Information in relation to the team behind the crypto can serve as a good pointer in respect of its long-term success. A found experienced and sound team of developers are good signs.

Check the Twitters of the teams, social media, and LinkedIn pages, also, YouTube interviews with team members.

Look at the team members' experience, generally speaking but also within the industry. Note whether it has developed something in the past; proof of work.

Also, note how much of the crypto the team holds and how much they have sold.

Note that a lot of projects will have anonymous teams and contributors. This is not necessarily a bad thing, but this will make assessing competency of the team harder.

Ask yourself:

1. Who is the team behind the crypto?
2. What experience do they have?
3. Do they have experience within the industry?
4. What other projects have they launched?
5. Have they been involved in any questionable projects or scams?

Roadmap

Good projects will have a vision and a roadmap. These can most often be found in the crypto's whitepaper or on its website. In the roadmap you can find upcoming features, or upgrades, new partnerships, or projects, events, or plans to improve the network.

Situation: If there is a healthy history of releases or upgrades, this is generally a good sign that the project can deliver what it promises about the crypto.

Ask yourself:

1. Does the project have a clearly defined roadmap?
2. What is their actual development timeline?
3. Are the goals realistic?

4. Does the crypto have a healthy history of feature releases or updates?

5. Have they fulfilled their promises?

6. What have they delivered so far? How has this affected adoption?

The problem

Does this project solves any problem that crypto is facing currently. Alternatively, is it creating a problem theoretically and then trying to solve it. Many times it is the latter case and hence no traction is gathered beyond hype.

Ask yourself:

1. Is this an important problem currently faced by crypto?

2. Is the project offering a solution to a real problem?

Sector/competition

In the crypto space, there are often many different projects trying to achieve similar goals. So one should look at the competitors of the project and compare them to it.

The whitepaper of the crypto should give a good indication. It's also useful to identify what other projects they are competing against and what existing infrastructure they are trying to replace or improve. Specifically, consider if the market is likely to be oversaturated with solutions that will reduce the need for adoption. Niche markets are small but the likelihood of adoption can be higher as a result.

What segment does the crypto belong to? Payment, NFTs, metaverse/gaming smart contract Layer 2 solutions, etc. All of these segments have functional projects, so one needs to see where the crypto stands about its direct competitors.

Looking into a crypto's competitors can be very enlightening. Crypto can look good on paper when one looks at it by itself, but taking it and putting it next to its competitors might show it to be weaker.

Ask yourself:

1. How many competitors are there?
2. How does the crypto compare to its competitors?
3. Is the product unique?
4. What long-term prospects are there in the sector?
5. What risks are facing this project?
6. What differentiates this project?

News/social media

Sound projects usually have a good online presence. This helps them to build a good community and advertise their product. This strength of the community can be gauged by the channels which the project has in social media. If a crypto does not have a decent online presence, then that's a red flag.

They go through the project's Twitter, Discord and Telegram channels. This shows them how the team relates to the community, and one gets to see what others say about it. Evidence of a real community working on and thriving helps add to an investor's confidence in a project.

Also, search LunaCrush and news websites and check to see if the project has suffered from any hacks or attacks.

Ask yourself:

1. How many social media followers does the project have?
2. What is the engagement like?
3. What is the general tone of the community?
4. Does the team engage with the community?
5. Has the project suffered from any hacks or attacks in the past?

Tokenomics

We touched upon some of the tokenomics you really should know about: supply, allocation/distribution, inflation, and utility. It's going to be helpful to have this checklist for applying your knowledge. As you're researching a token, try to find answers to each of these questions.

Supply

Looking beyond the supply of the crypto when searching through them, we want to see how the supply will change in the future, because this will ultimately determine if it will hold its value or increase or decrease in value over time.

Circulating supply

Issued so far - that is the number of tokens in the market; hence, that is the circulating supply.

How many of them are there right now? What's the circulating supply?

Maximum supply

Not all tokens have a fixed maximum supply. Comparing the circulating supply against the maximum supply indicate how many more are going to be released, which is an essential piece of information for considering the future value of a protocol. If the circulating supply is low, but the maximum supply is high, that's a red flag because it means your tokens may face dilution in their value.

- How many will ever exist in the future? (Is there a maximum supply?)
- How does the maximum supply compare to the circulating supply?
- How will the supply change over time? (Distribution schedule, covered later)

How will supply changes affect the token price?

It really just comes down to whether you think this protocol derives value over this time where tokens are being released that outweighs price pressure caused by these tokens being released. You might, for example, think that a project is likely to truly grow 10x in the next year and the circulating supply will 3x over that time period, at this time, this would nevertheless be good value.

Looking at the reverse of this, if you thought a project was only likely to grow by 50% in a year, and the circulating supply was going to increase by 40%, that would be much worse of an investment than the example above.

Market cap

The market cap or m'cap is the total dollar value of all coins in circulation. To total up the market cap of crypto, its circulating supply is multiplied by the token's price. Now, a crypto's market cap is far more coming into important than that token's $ price. Why? Because the price just does not say what a project is valued at. This method offers an indication of how valuable a crypto is, but also its growth potential.

What is the market cap of the crypto?

Is that a relatively small or large market cap compared to what it's worth, including growth prospects?

It's much easier to get massive returns from small market-cap coins since there is significantly more room to grow. A crypto with a smaller market cap is a riskier investment, though, since it's much more likely to go to 0 than a crypto with a larger market cap.

Fully diluted valuation

The fully diluted valuation, or FDV, is the theoretical market capitalization of the crypto in question if all tokens were to be in circulation. It's simply the case of multiplying the current price of that crypto by the maximum supply of tokens.

Do the math yourself and compare how the market cap looks compared to the fully diluted value. Massively different market caps and fully diluted values indicate there are many tokens just waiting to flood the market, and that should put you on alert.

What would be the theoretical mkt cap if all of the tokens were in circulation?

Is there a massive difference in the market cap of this token compared to its fully diluted valuation? In other words, are there still a lot of tokens to be released into the market?

If this is the case, is it going to be a problem?

How are the rest of the tokens going to be released, and when? See distribution below

This is important for obvious reasons, especially when taken in conjunction with distribution-that is to say, considering when and how the tokens will be released. Especially if you intend to be a long-term holder of a token, and its fully diluted value will likely be realized over that period, you can simply disregard the market cap entirely and take the fully diluted value at face value:

CoinGecko and Coinmarketcap are great websites to check the supply, trading volume, market cap, fully diluted value, price, and where you can buy crypto).

Block Explorers example. https://etherscan.io/, https://bscscan.com/, https://solscan.io/, and https://arbiscan.io/ are very useful for seeing a distribution of tokens, also max supply, holders, price, and fully diluted value. Find the token address on the project docs or CoinGecko and Coinmarketcap and search it in the relevant block explorer.

Distribution

Do your research on the distribution of the crypto: that means at what rate a token is released, where, to whom it is distributed, and how does that affect its value and reputation.

The concentration of tokens should be noted on few investors or team members, as this, in itself, is a high-risk factor. They can gain too much power of governance or manipulate the prices of tokens, pumping and dumping at will in their favor.

A good distribution design is the case when not a high percentage of the tokens are held by a person or group but rather are spread among many, with much focus on the community allocation. The distribution of tokens to the community incentivizes the protocol.

It has public and private numbers of tokens issued, and it has to point out the wallets with major tokens and decide whether they could be sold if the price went through the roof.

Remember that the velocity of token distribution also plays a role, meaning the Fully Diluted Value, or FDV, was the theoretical crypto mcap at an entirely in-supply token base. Look at the Supply and Market Capitalization in conjunction with the distribution rate.

The difference in both the terms is huge.

These tokens could be locked for some time, in which case they will not be able to be transacted or traded in the market. That's what a 'vesting schedule' really is. A good vesting schedule increases the confidence of token holders because it means the mass issue of tokens allocated to the team or private investors won't flood the market.

- Who gets how many tokens at launch?
- How were tokens distributed (fair launch, pre-mine, ICO, IEO etc)?
- How many tokens are allocated to team members?
- How fair does the distribution seem?
- Do a few wallets hold most of the tokens?
- How much of the supply can the community get hold of?

- How and when will new tokens be released?
- When will locked-up tokens be released? (What is the vesting schedule?) Will a lot of locked-up tokens be released at once?
- When are private investors unlocking?

Wallet holders

As, for example, on Etherscan-there are similar services for most blockchains-you just need to find the one relevant for your project: Solscan, Arbiscan etc. can see all wallets holding the token. Do your own research.

This allows you to go see which wallets retains a lot of the token. This is good since you can then see if one wallet retains a large amount of the supply, and therefor thus can dictate the price, or dump the token. Note, often the largest wallets is the protocols treasury, mining wallet, vesting contract or similar. So be sure to check ut the wallets before you make any rash conclusions.

Also, note that in case it is a governance token, such holders, provided their positions be big or large enough, may greatly influence the protocol's governance.

Check the project documents (tokenomics section) and information you can find through Google searches (be wary and cross-check sources).

Inflationary or deflationary?

A crypto's either inflationary or deflationary. Do your homework on inflations. It may decrease the value of a token over time; however, on the other hand, if the inflation gets implemented well, it could add huge value by attracting interest and liquidity that turbocharges growth.

With fewer tokens, each one is worth more; hence, such deflationary tokens may be highly valuable. In actual sense, it is introducing risk factors since it is pretty complex to get it right and when home wrong, this might just ruin a protocol; therefore, we must think of how, why, and when those tokens are being burnt.

Is the token inflationary or deflationary?

What is the inflation rate, and where are the emissions (new tokens) going?

Is the inflation rate due to reduce over time? This could mean the protocol is effectively bootstrapping liquidity in the early stages.

Are there plans for it to be deflationary? If so, what are they and how will it work?

Are there plans to stop emissions at a set point? What will happen after that? Will there be incentives for people to continue using the platform?

Check the project documents, search Google, and use sites like Duna Analytics.

Utility

It's also known, very often, as the token's use-case. Utility when looking for utility in a token ask yourself: why would I actually want to hold this token? Revenue sharing, staking, governance etc are some reasons. A token needs to have a good reason for existing, and people wanting to hold it.

Through revenue sharing, the token holders gain a percentage of the token's revenue. If rewards and revenue are actually built in through staking or some other form, it is far easier to justify investing in the token.

Governance means that the token holders are awarded a say in the decisions and about the direction of the project. Governance tokens gain the power to distribute power across the whole of a community.

Note that "utility tokens" and "token utility" are not the same thing. Token utility is the umbrella term for what a token does, a utility token is one of those use cases. Utility tokens can be good investments as long as they have clearly valuable utility.

- What is the token's purpose?
- What is its utility? What does it do?
- Is it a utility token?
- Is it governance (meaning is it used to decide what happens to the protocol)?
- Is it revenue sharing?
- What gives this token value as an investment?
- Does the token have built-in rewards?

Chapter 17

Technical Analysis

Technical analysis involves studying the historical price action of an asset to predict its future movements. It works because of factors such as investor behavior and crowd psychology. Investors often make decisions based on psychological biases. The efficiency of technical analysis is increased when most market players use similar tools, causing key price levels to overlap and creating a self-fulfilling prophecy. Recognizing patterns of repeated price movements can help investors gain an advantage in developing forward strategies or achieving returns.

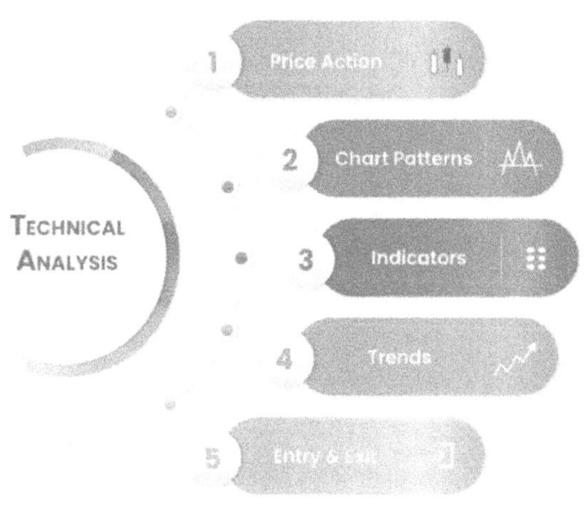

Source: Forex

Despite its relatively young age, the cryptocurrency market already exhibits patterns across short- and medium-term time frame. Understanding chart types, time frames, and psychological factors is essential. However, it is important to note that past performance does not guarantee future results. Technical analysis can tip the probabilities in your favor but does not promise profit, highlighting the need for sound risk management.

Gaining experience and skills in technical analysis is like learning to ski—you cannot become a professional skier by simply reading a book on the subject. Mastery of cryptocurrency technical analysis requires both direction and practice.

Line Charts

Line charts reflect only the closing prices of the market. For any given time period, you can know only what the crypto's price is at the end of that period, not the movements it experienced during that time. A line is drawn from one closing price to the next, allowing you to see the general movement of a currency pair over time.

Bar Charts

No, this option isn't a list of local drinking establishments! A bar chart shows you the opening market price, the price action during the time frame, and the closing price. The little horizontal line to the left indicates the opening price, while the line to the right marks the closing price.

Source: Investing.com

Candlestick Charts

Candlestick charts resemble bar charts, but the area between the open and close is colored to indicate market movement during that period. If the market moved up, indicating bullish sentiment, the area is usually colored green. If the market moved down, indicating bearish sentiment, the area is usually colored red. You can choose any colors you prefer, but green for bullish and purple for bearish are common choices. Candlestick charts also show the low and high prices the asset traded within that time frame.

Candlestick charts are my favorite not just because they are aesthetically pleasing but also because they were created by a Japanese rice trader. Having love for anime, I appreciate anything with Japanese roots, like Bitcoin's anonymous founder(s). Although nobody truly knows who founded Bitcoin, the creator(s) at least pretended to be Japanese and used the name Satoshi Nakamoto.

Bullish and Bearish Bars

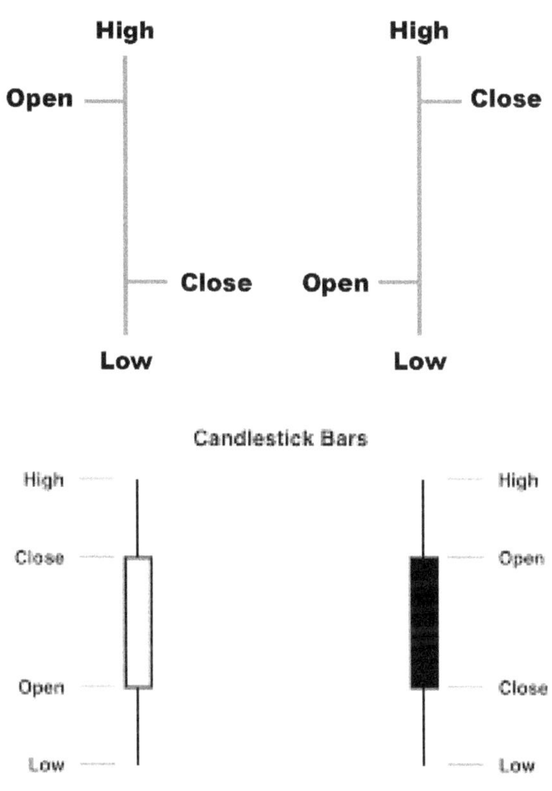

Identifying Key Levels

Technical analysis is an essential aspect of trading in cryptocurrencies. It involves examining past price data to identify patterns and trends that can project potential future price movements. The primary objective is to establish ideal prices for buying and selling cryptocurrencies. In this paper, we focus on two crucial concepts: support and resistance levels, and the use of Fibonacci retracement levels.

Support Levels

Support levels are significant price points where a cryptocurrency tends to stop falling and starts rising. They act as psychological barriers that the price cannot breach on the downside. The following methods can help identify and use support levels:

1. **Historical Data**: Analyze historical performance graphs to identify price points where the cryptocurrency has consistently stopped falling. These points indicate potential support levels.

2. **Psychological Hurdle**: Support levels represent price points where most investors believe the cryptocurrency is undervalued and should be bought, preventing further price declines.

3. **Strength of Support**: The more frequently a support level is tested and holds, the stronger it is. However, if a support level is broken, it can lead to a significant drop to the next support level.

Resistance Levels

Resistance levels are the opposite of support levels. They act as barriers that prevent the price from rising further. Traders use these levels to make selling decisions on existing holdings. The following methods can help identify and use resistance levels:

1. **Historical Peaks**: Observe previous peaks in the price chart. Any peak above the current market value is considered a resistance level.

2. **Psychological Barrier**: Resistance levels represent price points where most traders believe the cryptocurrency is overvalued and are willing to sell, forming a ceiling.

3. **Strength of Resistance**: Similar to support levels, the more frequently a resistance level is tested and holds, the stronger it is. Once broken, it can lead to a price surge to the next resistance level.

For instance, in 2021 and 2022, major resistance levels for Bitcoin were around $65,000, $59,000, and $47,000. These levels acted as barriers where the price struggled to rise further.

Moving Average Charts

Many investors find the details of price charts hard to navigate. Fortunately, moving averages simplify the process by highlighting sensible trends and aiding in well-informed trade decisions. Moving averages are widely used technical tools that smooth price data into a trend for a clearer definition of market direction. Below is an introduction to using moving averages and some sophisticated technical indicators to improve your trading:

Simple Moving Averages

Moving Averages (MAs) are mathematical calculations that average a series of prices over a defined period. They smooth out price data to help identify trends. There are several types of moving averages, each serving a unique purpose:

Simple Moving Average (SMA): This is the average price over a specified number of periods. For instance, a 15-day SMA calculates the average of the last 15 days' prices.

Exponential Moving Average (EMA): Similar to SMA but places more weight on recent prices, responding faster to new information.

Short-term vs. Long-term MAs

Short-term MAs (e.g., 15-day MA): These respond quickly to recent price changes and are used to identify short-term trends.

Long-term MAs (e.g., 200-day MA): These spot major trends and are less affected by short-term price fluctuations.

Technical analysts often use short-term and long-term MAs in combination to gain a more comprehensive understanding of market trends. For example, if a short-term MA crosses above a long-term MA, it signals a bullish trend. Conversely, if a short-term MA crosses below a long-term MA, it indicates a bearish trend.

Sophisticated Moving Averages and Indicators

For those interested in advanced technical analysis, the following tools can help provide more accurate market sentiment and potential price action.

Moving Average Convergence Divergence (MACD):

MACD is the difference between a short-term EMA and a long-term EMA.

A signal line, usually a 9-day EMA, is drawn to provide buy or sell signals. If the MACD crosses above the signal line, it implies a bullish trend; if it crosses below, it indicates a bearish trend.

Bollinger Bands:

Bollinger Bands consist of a middle band (SMA) and two outer bands representing standard deviations of the SMA.

These bands expand and contract based on market volatility. Prices tend to bounce within the bands, and moves outside the bands can indicate strong trends.

Relative Strength Index (RSI):

RSI is a momentum oscillator that measures the speed and change of price movements.

RSI values range from 0 to 100. An RSI above 70 usually indicates overbought conditions, while an RSI below 30 suggests oversold conditions.

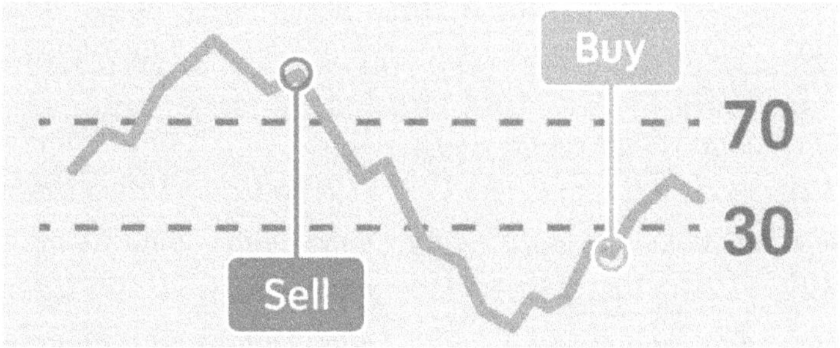

Ichimoku Kinko Hyo

The Ichimoku Cloud is a versatile indicator that combines various moving averages to provide a comprehensive view of ongoing market trends, as well as support and resistance levels.

There are five lines: the Tenkan-sen (conversion line), the Kijun-sen (base line), the Senkou Span A and Senkou Span B (together forming the cloud), and the Chikou Span (lagging line).

Practical Application

Combinatorial Indicators: Combining the best tools can be very useful. You can define the trend with MAs, gauge the degree of momentum with RSI, and measure volatility with Bollinger Bands. Your trading idea is more reliable if multiple indicators confirm the signals.

Example Strategy

Definition of Trend: Use long-term MAs, such as a 200-day SMA, to define the trend.

Spot Buy/Sell Signals: Look for crossovers in short-term MAs, such as the 15-day SMA crossing above or below the 50-day SMA.

Indicators Confirmation: Check for MACD convergence/divergence, RSI overbought/oversold levels, and Bollinger Bands volatility.

Moving averages and advanced technical indicators are essential tools for cryptocurrency traders navigating this highly volatile market. Knowing and applying these tools correctly helps identify trends, spot buying and selling signals, and confirm market sentiment, leading to more informed trade decisions.

- **Basic Moving Averages**: These smooth out price data to highlight trends.
- **Sophisticated Indicators**: These provide deeper insights into market momentum and volatility.
- **Combinational Tools**: Using multiple indicators together improves the accuracy of your strategy.

By combining these techniques, traders can develop a strong technical analysis toolkit, enhancing their profitability in the volatile cryptocurrency market.

Chapter 18

Getting Ahead of the Crowd: Investing in ICOs

Initial Coin Offerings (ICOs) are a method of fundraising for new cryptocurrency projects, similar to how start-ups raise capital. Here's a comprehensive guide to understanding and participating in ICOs.

Understanding ICOs

Definition and Purpose:

An ICO (Initial Coin Offering) is a crowdfunding method using Bitcoin, Ethereum, and other cryptocurrencies to raise funds for a new cryptocurrency project. The funds raised are intended for the development of a product or service associated with the new cryptocurrency.

How It Works:

Idea Generation: It begins with a unique idea for a cryptocurrency that can be applied to an existing product or an entirely new project.

Creation of White Paper: The project team publishes a white paper detailing the concept, technology, objectives, and roadmap of the new cryptocurrency.

Token Generation: New tokens, which are units of the new currency, are issued on a blockchain platform.

Public Announcement: The project is announced to potential investors using various marketing strategies.

Fundraising: Investors purchase the new tokens using existing cryptocurrencies like Bitcoin or Ethereum.

Development: The raised funds are used to develop the project as described and promised in the white paper.

Investing in an ICO:

Key Steps to Invest:

Research: Thoroughly research the project, including the team, technology, and market potential of the token.

Assessing the White Paper: Read and evaluate the white paper for feasibility, clarity, and credibility.

Background Check: Gather information about the project team, advisory board, and other key individuals involved.

Assessing Tokenomics: Study the distribution, use case, and supply of tokens.

Funding: Prepare the necessary cryptocurrencies, typically Bitcoin or Ethereum, to fund your investment.

Participate: Follow the instructions provided by the ICO, contribute funds, and claim your tokens.

Create Your Own ICO

How to Create an ICO:

Idea Creation: Define the purpose and vision of your new cryptocurrency.

White Paper Creation: Write a white paper that provides detailed information about the project, technology, roadmap, and tokenomics.

Token Creation: Choose a blockchain platform and design your tokens.

Legal Compliance: Ensure compliance with existing regulations and legal frameworks.

Marketing and Community Building: Advertise the ICO through various channels, engage with potential investors, and build a community around your project.

ICO Launch: Announce the ICO and clearly outline the steps for participation.

Development and Execution: Use the raised funds to develop the project as planned, and keep investors updated on progress.

ICOs vs. IPOs

Initial Coin Offerings (ICOs) and Initial Public Offerings (IPOs) are both methods of raising funds, but they differ significantly in process, accessibility, and what investors receive in return. Here is a detailed comparison:

Comparison Point	ICO (Initial Coin Offering)	IPO (Initial Public Offering)
Regulation	Typically less regulated, often falls under regulatory scrutiny as laws evolve.	Highly regulated by government entities like the SEC (U.S.).
Investor Requirements	Often open to the general public with fewer restrictions.	Generally restricted to accredited investors initially; broader public can invest post-IPO.
Ownership and Control	Investors receive tokens, which may not confer ownership rights.	Investors receive shares, representing ownership and voting rights in the company.

Knowing the ICO Investment Process:

Investing in an Initial Coin Offering (ICO) involves several steps, ranging from research and preparation to actual participation in the offering. Below is a brief outline of the ICO investment process:

1. Research and Preparation

Identify Suitable ICOs: Research and identify ICO projects that align with your investment goals and risk tolerance. Look for projects with a strong team, innovative technology, clear use cases, and a transparent white paper and roadmap.

Purchase Cryptocurrency: Most ICOs require investment in cryptocurrencies like Ethereum or Bitcoin. Purchase the necessary cryptocurrency from a reputable exchange and transfer it to your cryptocurrency wallet.

Create a Cryptocurrency Wallet: Secure a cryptocurrency wallet to store the tokens issued in the ICO. Since most ICOs are built on the Ethereum blockchain, you typically need an Ethereum-compatible wallet.

2. Registration for ICO

Visit Official ICO Page: Visit the official website or documentation of the ICO project to understand the terms, token sale details, and registration process.

Complete Due Diligence: Perform thorough due diligence on the ICO project by reviewing the white paper, the team's credentials, the roadmap, and community feedback. Verify the project's authenticity and assess its success probability.

Register for the ICO: Follow the registration instructions provided by the ICO project. This may involve submitting personal information, completing KYC verification, and accepting the terms and conditions of the token sale.

3. Participating in the ICO

Wait for Launch Date: Await the scheduled launch date of the ICO token sale. Stay updated with announcements from the ICO project team.

Transfer Cryptocurrency: On the launch date, transfer the required amount of cryptocurrency from your wallet to the specified public address provided by the ICO project. Be prepared to cover any associated transaction fee.

4. Post-ICO Process

Receive Tokens: After a successful transaction, wait for the ICO project team to distribute the purchased tokens to your cryptocurrency wallet. This might take some time, depending on the project's distribution schedule.

Monitor Investment: Keep track of your investment and the progress of the ICO project. Stay informed about project developments, partnerships, and market trends that could impact the value of your tokens.

Secure Your Tokens: Store your tokens in a secure cryptocurrency wallet. Follow best practices for private key management and wallet access.

By diligently following these steps, you can participate in ICOs and potentially invest in promising blockchain projects. Remember that ICO investments are speculative and come with risks, including regulatory uncertainty, project failure, and market volatility. Invest responsibly and seek professional advice if needed.

Chapter 19

Introducing Airdrops

In the cryptocurrency world, the term "Airdrop" refers to the public distribution of digital assets. Airdrops are a popular marketing technique, but they can also be used to make money.

Source: Coinswitch

What Are They Used For?

Airdrops have recently gained prominence as a marketing tool for crypto projects. They are used to enhance adoption and encourage community engagement by distributing new crypto tokens for free. This strategy drives awareness and quickly builds communities around the project.

How Do They Work?

Airdrops are typically distributed to members of a specific blockchain platform. Sometimes, recipients must hold particular tokens or maintain a minimum balance in their accounts to qualify. In other instances, they may need to perform simple tasks, such as posting about the project on social media platforms.

It's important to note that airdrops are not the same as ICOs. Initial Coin Offerings have been plagued by numerous scams, leading to heavy monitoring. Airdrops provide an alternative for development teams to release coins without using the ICO method.

NFTs & Airdrops

Airdrops are primarily used to reward early or loyal contributors to a project. Any type of token, whether fungible or non-fungible, can be airdropped. NFT projects can airdrop tokens, giving early users and contributors access to early minting opportunities.

Airdrop Risks

Airdrops come with associated risks, and it is crucial to be vigilant against dusting and phishing attacks. Be cautious when searching for information about exchanges or projects on Google. Fake websites often pay for advertisements on search engines and social media to lure victims.

Additionally, exercise caution when signing up for an airdrop. If an airdrop requires sending funds, it is almost certainly a scam. Some users create new wallets solely for airdrops to avoid being targeted by phishing and dusting attacks. Always remember to do your own research.

For a curated list of ongoing airdrop projects, regularly updated, visit Beyond Bitcoin Airdrops.

Keep a watch:

Here are some of the airdrop projects that made history.

1. Uniswap

2. Celestia

3. Arbitrum

4. Jupiter

5. Apecoin

Not financial advice, but these are just my personal favorites and are for learning purposes.

Part 6
CRYPTO STRATEGIES

Chapter 20

Spot Your Next Gems

Any Crypto strategies shared in this chapter are for educational purposes and are NOT FINANCIAL NOR INVESTMENT ADVICE. You are solely responsible for any capital-related decisions you make and the results of those decisions.

We are confident that those who identified the right altcoins at the beginning of the last bull-run are millionaires today. Here are our 10 rules that will help you discover your next gems.

Rule 1: New bull-run = new alts.

It's simple: don't buy old alts. Old altcoins have already peaked. Faith in them wanes as they become relics of the past. The market favors new, innovative, and hyped tokens. These new tokens hold more potential and are more likely to bring substantial gains compared to established altcoins.

Rule 2: ICOs and IDOs

During a bull run, participate in everything that can bring you money, even the riskiest plays. In the previous bull cycle, ICOs/IDOs were the best bets. Investing in tokens pre-listing, when the price is still to be determined, has yielded substantial profits for many people.

Rule 3: Check Prices

Just as you check the weather before going out, you should check a token's price chart before investing. If a token has already pumped and then stabilized, achieving similarly great returns is highly improbable compared to a token that hasn't pumped much yet.

Rule 4: watchout Investors

It's risky to invest in tokens whose entry price for VCs/angels is significantly lower than yours. When investors' tokens unlock and trade at 50x or 100x from their entry point, they are likely to dump their positions. It's best to avoid such tokens.

Rule 5: Circulating Supply

Avoid tokens with frequent unlocks and low circulating supply. Economics dictates that price is generated at the intersection of demand and supply. Increasing the supply without an equivalent increase in demand causes a price drop, making such tokens risky investments.

Rule 6: Market Cap

Compare a token's market capitalization (MC) with others. If the MC is too large, the token won't yield significant profits. For example, people love SOL, but it can't go x130 because its MC would exceed Bitcoin's current worth of $1.3 trillion. Use sites like The Coin Perspective to compare market caps and see how a token's price would change with another token's market cap.

Rule 7: Narratives

First, predict the narrative, then pick the token. In the crypto world, everything grows when something grows. Predict the prevailing narrative and select tokens aligned with it.

Rule 8: Utility

Evaluate a token's utility; don't buy just for the ticker. In meme-led bull markets, this might sound amusing, but it's essential to consider the token's practical value, merits, and potential for ecosystem or community growth.

Rule 9: VCs Supporting a Project

VC funds play a significant role in a project's success or failure. Look for tokens invested in by Tier 1 VCs. Information about VC investments is available at Crypto Fundraising and Crunchbase.

Rule 10: Don't forget about useful tools. Peek at it in our following chapter.

As you embark on your journey into the world of altcoins, here are my personal favorites that I'm keeping an eye on for the upcoming cycles.

- PATEX – Patex Ecsosystem
- PENDLE – Pendle Finance
- DUSK – Dusk Foundation
- OM – Mantra chain
- LTO – The LTO network
- GFI – Goldfinch
- POLYX – Polymesh Network
- HIFI – Hifi finance

- CUDOS – Cudos
- ALEPH – Aleph
- AR – Arweave
- NOS – Nosana
- PEAQ – Peaq Network
- IO – Ionet
- NATIX – Natix network
- AI – Sleepless AI
- NAVI – Atlas Navi
- GLQ – Graphlinq protocol
- ENQAI – Emerged – enqAI
- AQTIS – Aqtis
- PALM – Palm AI
- EMC – EMC protocol
- GPU – Node AI
- SPEC – Spectral Labs
- MOG – MOG
- HONEY – Honey
- GHOST – Ghost

Watchout:

If you are looking for the next altcoins to watch out for upcoming bull season 2024-2025 you made the right decision by purchasing this book. When you search for cryptocurrencies to buy most of the websites and influencers suggest those that have already made returns in the previous cycles or the projects they are associated with. Here are the genuine picks of those that personally keeping an eye on.

Cryptocurrency	Ticker	Narratives	Prices in $	Exchange
Entangle	NGL	DeFi	$0.67	Bybit
ChainGPT	CGPT	AI	$0.23	Bybit
Bittensor	TAO	AI	$401.20	Binance
Patex Ecosystem	PATEX	RWA	$4.41	Gate.io
Kaspa	KAS	Blockchain	$0.13	Binance
Mavia Game	MAVIA	GameFi	$3.08	Binance
Graphlinq	GLQ	AI	$0.10	Gate.io
Ondo Finance	ONDO	RWA	$1.18	Binance
Atlas Navi	NAVI	AI	$0.25	Gate.io
Star Heroes	STAR	GameFi	$0.31	Bybit
Orai Chain	ORAI	AI	$13.54	Gate.io

This cycle is all about Memes here is the list of meme tokens to watch out for:

- BRETT
- WIF
- POPCAT
- TRUMP
- PONKE
- MYRO
- BODEN
- FOXY

Chapter 21

Crypto Tools

Here is a list of 25+ crypto tools to help you make better investment decisions:

- **Glassnode**: Provides on-chain data and insights for crypto news.
- **Coinglass.com**: Offers TA tools required to analyze tokens (greed, funding, order books).
- **CoinMarketCap**: Provides various cryptocurrency prices and market capitalization data.
- **CoinGecko**: Another source for cryptocurrency prices and market capitalization data.
- **TradingView**: A social network for traders and investors with powerful charting tools for cryptocurrency markets.
- **Airdrops.io**: Lists the latest ongoing airdrop projects.
- **Airdropalert**: Another platform that lists the latest ongoing airdrop projects.
- **CoinMarketCal**: The leading economic calendar for crypto assets.
- **ArkhamIntel**: Provides on-chain wallet interactions.
- **CryptoQuant.com**: Offers on-chain data.
- **IntoTheBlock**: A platform providing detailed blockchain analytics and intelligence.

- **Messari Crypto**: Delivers high-quality data and research for transparency in the crypto economy.
- **DEXToolsApp**: Provides graphs of DeFi projects.
- **52kskew**: A data analytics and trade execution platform for cryptocurrency derivatives.
- **Chain Analysis**: A blockchain analysis tool used for compliance and investigation.
- **DuneAnalytics**: A tool for querying, visualizing, and sharing Ethereum blockchain data.
- **ICODrops**: A calendar of active and upcoming ICOs and IEOs.
- **Nansen.ai**: Analyzes blockchains to deliver actionable insights in the DeFi space.
- **DefiLlama**: Provides comprehensive DeFi metrics.
- **L2Beat**: Offers L2 data and total value locked (TVL).
- **TokenTerminal**: Provides token financials and revenue tracking.
- **The Block**: Delivers news and research reports.
- **CryptoPanic.com**: Aggregates crypto news.
- **Cointelegraph**: For detailed crypto news and analysis.
- **SantimentFeed**: Helps analyze market sentiment.
- **LunarCrush**: Provides token trends and social mentions.
- **OnChainFX**: Offers a comprehensive view of the cryptocurrency market, including real-time prices, market capitalization, and historical data.
- **Binance Research:** Binance's research arm provides in-depth analysis and reports on cryptocurrencies, blockchain projects, and market trends. It offers insights into market sentiment, token economics, and regulatory developments.

- **TokenAnalyst:** Specializes in blockchain data analytics, focusing on transaction flows, wallet movements, and liquidity analysis across various blockchains. It provides insights into market trends and investor behavior.

Think about This:

My Anti- To Do List

1. Do not invest your money into a project even if the reward/risk is high.

   You should always conduct your own research and spend time to understand if the project is worth your money.

2. Do not evaluate your results on daily basis

   Always asses your success in a bigger picture (monthly, Quarterly, Yearly)

3. Do not be emotionally attached.

4. Always be open to reconsider your investments.

5. Do not underestimate the power of market reacting to news.

6. The most important principle is Do not count your chickens before they hatch.

Chapter 22

Ultimate Secret Tools

DEX Scanner

Let's demystify the mysteries hidden in Dexscreener's code. While over 10,000,000 people use this tool daily, only 1% truly master it.

Source: Dexscanner

Step 1: Choosing the Preferred Network

Navigate to Dexscreener.com. The $SOL network has been exceptionally hot and will soon be succeeded by $BASE.

Step 2: Properly Selecting Tokens

Focus on two key sections to discover early gems:

Gainers 24h

New Pairs 24h

These filters may appear simple but can uncover tokens with potential gains of 10-100X.

Step 3: Deep Exploration with DEX Screener

This platform provides comprehensive information about each token, helping you differentiate between gems and lesser assets:

- Token market cap
- Total transactions
- Project socials
- Largest token holders
- Top traders
- Liquidity providers
- Token charts

Step 4: Viewing Multiple Token Charts

Efficiently monitor up to 16 charts simultaneously in the "Multicharts" section. This feature streamlines tracking without the need to check each play individually.

Step 5: Observing Portfolios, Influencers, Insiders, and Whales

In the "Portfolio" section, manage all your assets and track their acquisition dates. You can also monitor other portfolios to see which tokens influencers and insiders are accumulating.

Let's make 1000x

Everyone knows that altseason is inevitable, and all we need to make significant returns is a good amount to invest, a year of Bull Run, and this book that contains the blueprint. Here's the most effective way to research altcoins and find opportunities.

1. DYOR (Do Your Own Research) on Altcoins Ranked 100-500 by Market Cap

    - **Visit Websites**: Use platforms like CoinGecko, CryptoRank, and CoinMarketCap.
    - **Filter Alts**: Focus on sectors you are interested in or based on your risk appetite.
    - **Identify Potential Projects**: Look for altcoins that are currently declining but showing significant building progress and have a strong community.
    - **Add to Watchlist**: Compile a list of all potential projects for further analysis.

2. Analysis of the Project's Team

   - **Team Interest**: Ensure the team is genuinely interested in the project's growth and its community.
   - **Active Development**: Check if the team is actively working on the project, providing updates, and engaging with the community.

3. Tokenomics

   - **Official Website:** Visit the project's official website to find detailed documentation and tokenomics.
   - **Valuable Insights**: Look for hidden insights that others might overlook.
   - **Project Goals**: Examine the project's goals and the team's progress towards achieving them.

4. Buying the Tokens

   - **Research Listings:** Use CoinGecko, CryptoRank, and CoinMarketCap to check which centralized exchanges (CEXs) or decentralized exchanges (DEXs) list the project.
   - **Purchase Tokens:** Visit those exchanges and buy the tokens.

5. Have a Clear Take-Profit Strategy Before Investing

   - **Entry and Exit Plan:** Know when you'll buy and when you'll close positions to avoid trading based on luck.
   - **Example Strategy:** Sell 50% of your holdings when the price doubles. If the asset rises quickly and the trend is bullish, consider selling 20% or 25% instead

Think about This:

What are the five things you are going to take away from this book?

You've got this!

Be optimistic. Be confident.

Just remember – "Comparison is the thief of Joy".

Everyone's journey is different

Enjoy your journey into the world of cryptocurrencies! I hope this book has provided you with valuable insights into cryptocurrencies and helped you determine if this is the right investment segment for you. Congratulations on taking your first step by choosing this book, which costs less than a meal. You're already among the top 5% of the population who are involved in the crypto space.

Regulations

The regulations relating to cryptocurrencies within India have been a topic of much debate and have seen constant evolution over the years. The government of India has often taken the middle path by allowing innovation but not at the cost of proper regulation. Over the past few years, India has slowly been working on designing a regulatory framework- that deals with the risks and benefits associated with such currencies.

Although the RBI initially banned banks from trading in cryptocurrencies way back in 2018, the ban was subsequently overturned by the Supreme Court in 2020. Since then, sustained efforts have been made to come up with a broad regulatory framework on the matter. In 2021, the government introduced the Cryptocurrency and Regulation of Official Digital Currency Bill, which is a law that would seek to impose a ban on all private cryptocurrencies while at the same time providing support for the coming of a CBDC.

Though these discussions are in progress, the operative word, as of mid-2024, is uncertainty-the detailed guidelines being worked out by the government and financial regulators.

The government is waiting with bated breath for further regulatory clarity, as indeed, cryptocurrency exchanges and users in India, or for that matter, the future of digital assets in this country, is going to hangs a great deal on this aspect.

Disclaimer

None of the information provided in this book is intended for educational or informative purposes and should not be construed as financial, legal, or specific advice. The content is based on the author's research, critical analysis, personal reviews, and is subject to change without notice. Readers are strongly urged to independently verify such information through a licensed financial advisor and seek legal counsel before making any investment decisions.

The author and publisher do not guarantee the accuracy, applicability, fitness, or completeness of the contents presented in this book. All recommendations made herein are without guarantee. Neither the author nor the publisher shall be liable for any physical, psychological, emotional, financial, or commercial damages, including but not limited to special, incidental, consequential, or other damages.

4 Critical Disclaimers:

1. **Not a Finance Expert:** I am not a finance expert. I trust your knowledge and judgment, and I encourage you to conduct your own research before acting on any information provided in this book.

2. **Non-Promotion Statement:** I have mentioned numerous companies, projects, brands, websites, and applications in this book. None of them are aware of being mentioned, and none have paid me for promotion. I personally use many of these services and have made personal investments in them.

3. **Personal Experience Disclaimer:** Everything I share in this book is based on my personal experiences and perspectives. What has worked for me may not necessarily work for you, and I acknowledge and respect individual differences.

4. **Source and Purpose:** Much of the content and ideas in this book are sourced from various websites, books, articles, and other publications. The primary goal of "Beyond Bitcoin: Unlocking the Secrets of Cryptocurrency" is to simplify and explain a wide range of concepts and technical terms related to cryptocurrency.

Objective: The main objective of this book is to serve as a guide to understanding cryptocurrency concepts and terminology. My intention is to showcase possibilities rather than prescribe actions. Ultimately, your path in the crypto world will be unique to you and chosen by you.

Scan the QR code to access the links mentioned in this book, free tools, and frequent updates.